Get Set for
Reading

Continental

Credits

Illustrations: Pages 7, 11, 20, 23, 29, 31, 33, 46, 69, 75, 78, 107, 110, 145, 159, 164: Laurie Conley; Page 38: Margaret Lindmark; Page 42: Harry Norcross; Page 108: David Stirba

Photos: Page 20: Image used under Creative Commons from Cburnett; Page 26: Image used under Creative Commons from Martin Holst Friborg Pedersen; Pages 49, 119: © Royalty-Free/Corbis; Page 56: © Bettman/Corbis; Page 65: Image courtesy of T. Piper, NOAA OE; Page 87: Image used under Creative Commons from Tiago Fioreze; Pages 92, 174: NASA; Page 96: Official White House Photo by Sonya N. Hebert; Page 97: Official White House Photo by Pete Souza; Page 98: www.letsmove.gov; Page 102: © Copyright Eastman Kodak Company; Page 103: www.photos.com; Page 127: Carol M. Highsmith's America, Library of Congress, Prints and Photographs Division, LC-DIG-highsm-04261; Page 128: Journalist 2nd Class Todd Stevens; Page 133: www.istockphoto.com/rsmseymour; Page 136: Personnel of NOAA Ship DELAWARE II; Page 140: NOAA/Department of Commerce; Page 141: NASA's Goddard Space Flight Center/Axel Mellinger; Page 146: PhotoLink; Page 164: Doug Menuez; Page 165: Image used under Creative Commons from Bruce McAdam; Page 166: Image used under Creative Commons from normanack; Page 170: NOAA's National Weather Service (NWS) Collection; Page 178: www.istockphoto.com/WillSelarep; Page 179: © Corel Corporation

Table of Contents

Get Set for Reading will help you prepare for reading tests. The reading comprehension skills you are learning now build on the comprehension skills you learned last year. Next year, you will continue building on your comprehension skills. Each year, you must take tests to show what you have learned. It is important to be ready for these tests by practicing and reviewing what you have learned.

This book focuses on the most important reading comprehension skills for Grade 4. There are units of lessons in this book. Each lesson reviews one type of text and the reading skills needed to understand that text. There are Focus Lessons at the beginning of the book to help you recall the skills needed to understand the different types of texts. The Focus Lessons explain important words and ideas.

Each Focus Lesson includes practice questions. First, you will read the passage. Then, there is a set of short-response questions that will help you think about the passage and its meaning. Read each question and think about the answer. There are answer explanations to help guide you to a correct answer.

Each lesson has a Guided Practice section. Here you will do more practice problems to determine your understanding of the text. Again, there are short-response questions to help you think about the passage.

Finally, there are Independent Practice questions. In this section, you will work on your own to answer multiple-choice questions about the passage.

At the end of the book is a glossary. The glossary will help you to review key words found throughout the lessons.

Focus Lesson

When you take a test, you might be asked to read a story and answer questions about it. Sometimes what you read is **nonfiction**—a story that is true. Other times, it is **fiction**—a made-up story. A literary story is one kind of made-up story. It has characters in it who speak to each other. It has a beginning, middle, and end.

There are many different kinds of literary stories. **Realistic fiction** is a made-up story that could happen in real life. **Traditional stories** teach a lesson. These include myths, fables, fairy tales, and folktales. **Myths** are stories that come from many cultures. Some of the best-known myths are those of the ancient Greeks and Romans. The main purpose of a myth is usually to try to explain how the world began, why things happen, or the customs of people. **Fables,** such as "The Tortoise and the Hare," are short stories that often have animals that act like humans. They usually teach a lesson about how people behave. **Fairy tales** have elements of magic. They often include creatures like giants, wicked witches, and elves. **Folktales** are stories about ordinary people that teach a lesson about how people behave. **Tall tales** wildly exaggerate the skills or strengths of the hero. The hero is usually a character from America's past like Paul Bunyan, a giant lumberjack.

Characters, plot, and setting all make up a good story. The **characters** are the people in the story, and the way they think, feel, and act help move along the plot. The **plot** is the order of events in a story. It is the **conflict,** or problem, that makes the story exciting. The **setting** is when and where the story takes place. It helps shape the characters and determines what they do. A story may be realistic fiction, a fairy tale, folktale, or even told as a poem, but it will always include characters, plot, and setting.

Read this story and answer the questions that follow.

Jason and the Golden Fleece

I think Jason is going to take the Golden Fleece when the dragon is not looking

1   Jason's father was the rightful heir to the throne of the city of Lolcus in Greece. But to regain his place as king, he must have the golden fleece. Jason went to the king who had it and said, "You must give me the golden fleece." The king did not give it to him but said, "Come again and I will consider your demand." *The King did not give the GF to Jason*

2   Then the king's daughter, Medea, said to Jason, "If you want the golden fleece, you must take it; my father will never give it to you. But there is a dragon dwelling beside the tree where the golden fleece hangs, and he never sleeps. He is always hungry and swallows anyone who comes near. No one can kill him, but I can make him sleep. He is very fond of cakes, so I will make his favorite cakes and add a special herb that will make the dragon sleep."

3   So Medea made the cakes and Jason took them to the dragon. When the dragon opened his huge jaws to swallow Jason, he instead received delicious cakes. The dragon ate them all and went to sleep. Then Jason climbed over the dragon and took the nail out of the tree. He put the golden fleece under his coat and ran to his ship, the Argo. Medea went with him and became his wife.

medea will help Jason by making cakes for the dragon that will make it sleep

4   But how angry the king was when he discovered that the golden fleece was gone! And his daughter was gone, as well!

5   The king sent his men in ships to take Jason, but they could not capture him. At last Medea and Jason and his men arrived in Greece. Jason's father was there, but he was a very old and sickly man by then. Jason asked Medea to use her magic to make the old man young again.

6   Medea took her carriage and flew through the air and did not come back for nine days. She picked flowers from the hills and found a variety of stones, which she needed for her potion. When she went home, she put all these things into a pot and cooked them.

7   When the potion was ready, she put a stick into the pot and watched as leaves immediately grew on it. Some of the juice fell on the ground and the grass grew up as high as her knee. So Medea knew the brew would make things grow.

A **narrator** is the person telling the story. The narrator may be a character or a person outside the story. A **first-person narrator** tells the story from his or her point of view using the words *I* and *we*. A **third-person narrator** uses characters' names or *he, she,* or *they.*

What type of narrator does this story have?

The **theme** of a story is its message. Characters, setting, dialogue, and plot help you figure out a story's theme.

What is this story's theme?

8   Jason's father went to sleep, and Medea put some of the juice into his mouth. His white hair suddenly turned black, and strong new teeth grew in his mouth. When he woke up, he looked and felt like a young man.

9   Jason's father lived many years as king. In time, his son took over the throne.

Focus Lesson: LITERARY TEXT

1   Part A

What problem does Jason have in the (beginning) of the story?

The problem was that the king would not give Jason the golden fleece.

my hint

> Reread paragraph 1. What is Jason trying to do? Jason must get the golden fleece so his father can take his rightful place as king.

Part B

How does Jason solve his problem?

Medea made some sleeping cake to make the dragon go to sleep. then

> Reread paragraphs 2 and 3. Who helps Jason solve the problem from Part A? What do they do? Jason gets help from Medea. After the dragon goes to sleep, he takes the golden fleece and escapes in his ship.

Focus Lesson

Poetry uses musical language to create pictures and words in your mind. Poems are made up of one or more **stanzas,** or **verses.**

Many poets use **figurative language** to help you see or feel language. Similes, metaphors, and personification are examples of figurative language. Sometimes a poem will repeat the same or similar beginning consonant sound in a line. This is called **alliteration.** Poets can also add sound words to their writing. Words that imitate sounds, such as *boom* and *crash,* are examples of **onomatopoeia.**

A **narrative poem,** like a story, has characters and a plot. It has a beginning, a middle, and an ending. Another kind is a **lyric poem,** which captures a moment or a feeling. Sometimes poems repeat sounds at the ends of words. This is called **rhyme.** Sometimes the rhyme comes at the end of a line of poetry.

> It's raining, it's **pouring,**
> The old man is **snoring;**

Sometimes the rhyming words appear in the same line.

> Jack and **Jill** went up the **hill**

A **limerick** is a short, silly poem usually made for fun. Limericks are filled with rhymes and have a bouncy rhythm. **Rhythm** is a pattern of stressed and unstressed beats in a line.

> There **was** an old **man** with a **flute,**
> A **serpent** ran **into** his **boot;**
> But he **played** day and **night,**
> Till the **serpent** took **flight,**
> And **avoided** that **man** with a **flute.**

Free verse is a kind of poetry with no rhythm or rhyme. You can put words together in any way to create a free verse poem.

Read this poem and answer the questions the follow.

Night Voyage

voygre is a trip

1. They flew like the night-wind flew, softly,
Sweet dusk sounds the water sang,
They came to a place in the shallows
And saw beautiful treasures at hand.
There was one lonely sycamore standing
On the wide empty island below,
2. It stood low on the edge of the water
It was swaying in sadness alone.
The clouds moved in silence above them
Like a fleet of drifting ghost ships.
3. And they floated on air like a feather
To an island of dreams, all the six.

A **simile** uses the words *like* and *as* to compare two things that are very different. A **metaphor** compares two things that are different but does not use *like* or *as*.

What is an example of a simile in this poem?

Personification makes something that is not human seem like a person in some way.

What is an example of personification in this poem?

1   **Part A**

What is an example of alliteration in the poem?

one exmaple of alliteration is that
the tree swaying sadness
alone.

> Reread line 2. What sound is repeated in this line? The *s* sound is repeated:
> "Sweet dusk sounds the water sang."

Part B

How does the use of alliteration from Part A help to enhance the poem?

the alliteration enhane the poem
because alliteration make you having
feelings. my feeling are sad
because tree was alone.

> Read line 2 again. How does saying this line make you feel? The repeated *s*
> sound focuses your attention on line 2 and helps to create the rhythm of the
> poem. It also helps give a soothing tone to the poem.

Focus Lesson

People are often entertained by **plays** and **drama**—stories written to be performed on a stage. Drama has been written for radio, movies, and television, too. Dramatic writing uses special features that give instruction to directors and performers for making the story come alive.

A **play** is a story that is performed by actors on a stage. A play is divided into **acts,** like a book is divided into chapters. Acts may be divided into **scenes.** A scene is part of the action that happens in one place.

Characters are the people who have parts in a play. A list of these characters is called the **cast.** The cast always appears at the beginning of a printed play or in the program. The name of the actor who plays each part follows the character's name. Sometimes there is a **narrator** who describes events in the play to the audience or reader.

Stage directions explain how actors should move and speak. In a **script,** or written version of the play, these stage directions are usually printed in *italics* and put inside parentheses, like this: (*laughing*).

Dialogue includes all the words characters speak in a play. In a script, dialogue comes directly after the character's name and any stage directions.

The writer explains when and where the story takes place, how the stage should look, who the characters are, and what the characters do or say.

The Wish-Bird

Cast of Characters:

Bird

Prince

Nurse

Scene I

The Prince and his Nurse walk in the palace gardens a few years ago.
A Bird is flying among the trees.

Prince: I am tired of the gardens, Nurse.

Nurse: Look at your pretty flowers, dear Prince.

Prince: I am tired of the flowers, as well.

Nurse: Look at your pretty doves, dear Prince.

Prince: I am tired of my doves, for I see them every day.

Nurse: Then look at your white, white rabbits, Prince.

Prince: I am tired of my rabbits, which do the same things always.

Nurse: Dear me! Dear me!

Prince: What is there new for me to look at, Nurse?

Nurse: I do not know, dear Prince.

Prince: *(shouting)* You must tell me what to look at, or I will send you to the king.

Nurse: Do not send me to the king, dear Prince!

Prince: Then tell me what to look at.

Bird: Look at me, Prince! Look at me!

Prince: Where are you?

Bird: I am in the cedar tree.

Nurse: It is the Wish-Bird, Prince!

Bird: Make a wish, Prince. I will give you what you ask for. But do not ask too much!

> The **setting** is where and when a play takes place. Many times, scenes in a play take place in different settings.
>
> *What is the setting of this scene?*

Prince: I wish these flowers were feathers!

Bird: Flowers, flowers, to feathers change!

Prince: *(shouting)* Look, Nurse, look! The flowers have changed to feathers! Let me wish again, Wish-Bird!

Bird: Make a wish. I will give you what you ask for. But do not ask too much!

Prince: *(shouting)* I wish my rabbits with wings could fly!

Bird: Rabbits, rabbits, fly with wings!

Prince: *(laughing)* Ha, ha! My rabbits now have wings! Let me wish again, Wish-Bird!

Bird: Make a wish. I will give you what you ask for. But do not ask too much!

Prince: I wish to have the moon, I do! I must have the moon!

Bird: Do not ask too much, Prince!

Prince: *(shouting)* I wish to have the moon, I say! Do you hear, Wish-Bird? I wish to have the moon!

Bird: You ask too much! Feathers, feathers, fly away!

Nurse: Prince, Prince, your feather flowers are flying away!

Bird: Rabbits, rabbits, fly away!

Nurse: *(crying)* Prince, Prince, your pretty rabbits are flying away!

Prince: *(shouting)* I want my pretty flowers, I do! I want my pretty rabbits, too!

Bird: You asked too much, Prince! You asked too much!

Prince: What will the king say?

Nurse: Dear me! Dear me! The king loved the flowers and white, white rabbits.

Prince: *(crying)* What shall I do, Wish-Bird?

Bird: Go plant flower seeds and care for them until they grow to flowers. Go feed your doves and care for them. Go work and work and work and never ask too much. Then someday I will come to you and you may wish again.

The Wish-Bird flies away.

Props are objects, such as books or plates, that are used by the characters on the stage. **Scenery** is the background and larger props that create the setting.

What is a prop that could be used in this play?

---

1   Part A

What does the prince do near the end of the scene that affects the ending?

_____

_____

_____

_____

> Reread the play. What is the one thing the prince does that the bird tells him not to do? The prince asks for the moon even though the bird warned him not to ask for too much.

Part B

How is the answer to Part A related to the theme of the play?

_____

_____

_____

_____

> The theme is a story's message. What does this play teach? The prince asked for too much and lost all the things he wished for. Don't be greedy in what you wish for.

2   Part A

How does the setting help explain what props and scenery should be in the scene?

_____

_____

_____

_____

> Look at the setting at the beginning of the scene. What objects should be on the stage? The setting is the palace gardens, with flowers and rabbits and a bird. The setting provides a place for the prince and his nurse to walk and see the familiar flowers and rabbits.

Part B

How does the dialogue between the characters depend on the setting?

_____

_____

_____

> Reread the conversation between the prince and the nurse. What are they talking about? The prince and the nurse are talking about what they see in the garden. The setting is the center of the action because the prince is bored and wants the garden to change.

Reading Literary Text   17

Narrative Text

Focus Lesson

Narratives are true stories about something that happened in history, a current event, or the story of a person's life. They are about real people and real events. A **biography** is a narrative written to inform a reader about someone. It is written by a person *other* than the subject. An **autobiography** is a narrative written by a person about his or her *own* life. Narrative text should show the reader what is happening or what someone is feeling rather than telling the reader.

When you read any kind of text, you may guess what is going to happen. When you do this, you are making a **prediction.** To make a good prediction, put clues together in the story with what you already know.

The author of a narrative usually gives his or her **point of view,** or opinion. This means that the author tells you what he or she thinks is most important. How do you know if you are reading facts or the author's opinions? A **fact** is something that you can be sure of. It can be proven. An **opinion** tells you how someone feels. Look for words such as *best, worst, always,* and *never.* These can mean the author is not using facts.

When you read, it is important to think about who is telling the story and why it is being told. In some texts, a character tells the story. This is called **first-person point of view.** The characters use the pronouns *I* and *we.* Other stories are told from the **third-person point of view.** The narrator uses the words *he, she,* and *they.* The viewpoint may depend on the **author's purpose** for writing. When two people have different reasons for writing, their writing shows different points of view.

Read this passage and answer the questions that follow.

Saving the Jaguar

A title or **heading** helps you predict what a text will be about.

What does the title tell you about this passage?

Kate Wheeler works for the Wildlife Conservation Society (WCS). She has helped in the efforts to save many animals on the endangered list. But her real passion is big cats. Kate works mainly on saving jaguars. Here, Kate talks about her work and how she feels about it.

Interviewer: Kate, when did you first become interested in big cats?

Kate: My family has always had both cats and dogs. I guess I just grew up loving animals. In fact, my parents ran an animal shelter just outside of Dallas. I used to work there in the summers. But I started learning about big cats in high school. I was on a field trip to a wild animal park. We heard a speech about the awful situation big cats were facing. I realized that both little cats and big cats need help to survive.

Interviewer: I see you have a special love for the jaguar. What is so special about this animal?

Kate: First, I think jaguars are one of the most amazing cats in the world. I feel each big cat is important to the earth. But jaguars are also what we call "umbrella species." They sit at the top of a complex system. If the jaguar is lost, much of the diversity of an area will be lost. The loss of one type of animal greatly affects all the others around it. That's why I love what I do. I feel I'm not only helping big cats. I'm helping the earth as well.

Interviewer: How did the jaguars get in so much trouble?

Kate: These cats are known for their beautiful spotted coats. In the 1960s, about 18,000 jaguars were killed each year just for their coats. Since then, the jaguar has done a little better. But poaching, or killing that is against the law, does still occur around the world.

Writers may not tell you everything. They want you to figure out some details based on what you know and what you are reading. This is called making inferences.

How does Kate probably feel about her job?

Interviewer: Is that the only reason jaguars are in trouble?

Kate: Oh, no. Jaguars need a lot of land to roam and hunt. Lots of people have moved into the jaguar's habitat. This threatens the cats' hunting grounds. People often bring animals. We've had the most trouble with cattle ranchers. Jaguars look at the cattle as food. This makes them a perfect target for hunters.

Interviewer: What is being done to help jaguars?

Kate: We've really done some great things! The first ever jaguar reserve was formed in Belize. This is a place where jaguars can live safely without the threat of hunters. Also, it has now become illegal to sell or trade jaguar skins.

Interviewer: What will you be doing to help jaguars in the next few years?

Kate: I'm very excited about this! I'll be working with the WCS to help create special forest areas. We call them "corridors." These areas should prevent the jaguar habitat from breaking apart.

Interviewer: Can we do anything to help?

Kate: You sure can! Tell your friends about conservation. Remember, saving a big cat helps save its habitat, too! Learn about big wild cats. They are wild for a reason and should never be kept as pets. And don't ever buy products made from real fur. This only adds to the problem.

1   Part A

What are two words that best describe Kate Wheeler?

_____

_____

_____

_____

> Reread Kate's answers to the questions. She shows that she is a caring person by talking about wanting to take care of animals and the earth. Kate is also enthusiastic because she seems excited about everything they are doing to help jaguars.

Part B

What are two sentences from the passage that support your answer to Part A?

_____

_____

_____

_____

> Reread Kate's first and fifth answers. Kate's first answer shows her caring: "I guess I just grew up loving animals." Kate's fifth answer shows her excitement: "We've done some great things!"

Focus Lesson

Recipes, directions, user guides, and forms are all examples of **instructional text.** They teach you how to do something, such as how to bake a cake, how to take great pictures, or how to plant a garden.

An instructional text should list the materials, equipment, or ingredients you need to complete a project. Knowing the materials you need helps you follow the directions. The **directions,** or steps, of a project need to be completed in the right order to get the correct result.

Many instructional texts have charts, maps, and pictures to help you learn from what you read. These **text features** give you extra information and clues that make it easier to understand what you are reading.

Read this passage and answer the questions that follow.

Make a Nature Trail Guide!

Making a nature trail guide is a great project for your classroom. Many people walk nature trails without really stopping to see, hear, smell, and feel what is around them. Your guide can highlight all the facts, details, and simple beauty of the trail. Here's how:

Materials
- photographs and illustrations
- colored paper
- pens, colored pencils, or markers
- scissors
- glue
- stickers or other flat decorations

Numbers or special symbols point out items on a list.

What do the bullets (•) in this passage list?

1   Use lots of photos and illustrations. You can scan them, draw them, or use clip art. Use these items to show readers what certain animals and plants look like. You may want to point out a plant to avoid, like poison ivy.

2   Make your guide informative but not too wordy. Don't bog down your readers with too much text. Simply note special features along the trail. Include facts and details that will make the reader's walk more enjoyable.

3   Refer to certain signs along the trail. These signs often refer to items in that spot. For example, *This maple tree is known as a home to lots of squirrels. Blue jays nest in this tree every summer.* (This would be a great place to show a picture of a squirrel or a blue jay. This way, readers will know what to look for.)

4   Add something for visitors to do at each stop. This will make them slow down and look around them. They will start to notice things they haven't before. They might even learn something new! For example, *Feel the soft leaves of this lamb's ear plant. Take a moment to smell the sweet scent of wild lavender.*

5   Now it's time to check all your facts. Ask yourself questions such as, "Have you named all plants and animals correctly?" "Have you identified plants that people should not touch?"

6   Print your brochures on colored paper and laminate them, if possible. This will make them last longer.

An **illustration,** or picture, does not *tell* you how or when something happened. It can help you see the way something should look.

What does the illustration in this passage show?

1   Part A

What is the purpose of this article?

_____

_____

> Look at the title and the first paragraph again. What is the article about? The article gives instructions for how to make a nature trail guide.

Part B

Think about the purpose of the article from Part A. What are three things the author did to achieve this purpose?

_____

_____

_____

> The purpose of the article is to explain how to make a nature trail guide. To do this, the author gives step-by-step directions for making a guide, shows a bulleted list of materials you need to make the guide, and shows a picture of a completed guide as a sample.

Focus Lesson

Expository text is nonfiction writing that informs, explains, describes, or defines a subject. Textbooks, guides, newspapers, and magazine articles are all examples of expository text. When you read, especially articles about school subjects, you may not know every word you see. But you can often figure out the meaning of a new word from other words near it in a sentence or paragraph. These words are **context clues.** Examples, descriptions, or synonyms can be used as context clues.

As you read, think about how events flow. The order in which events happen is called **sequence.** Sometimes **directions,** or a sequence of steps, is shown as a list with numbers or bullets. Look for sequence clue words, like *first, next, last, before, finally, now, after,* and *then.*

You may also want to understand why things happen. You can ask yourself, "Why did this happen?" That is the **cause.** Then ask, "What happened?" This is the **effect.** Look for clue words that signal causes: *if, because,* and *since.* These clue words signal effects: *then, so* and *that is why.*

Sometimes you may read two articles about the same subject, or you may read one article that talks about common subjects. As you read, you should **compare** the texts or subjects. How are they alike? Also, **contrast** the texts or subjects. Think about how they are different.

Sometimes when you read, you are looking for a **solution** to a **problem.** First, you need to identify what the problem is. Then you must find a solution that matches the problem. Look for words such as *because, since,* and *therefore* to help pick out a problem and its possible solution.

Read this passage and answer the questions that follow.

A Show of Sharks

1   Last Saturday, beachgoers at Sandy Beach were enjoying a beautiful, sunny day. But shortly past noon, Lauren Cline spotted something in the water. "I was watching some friends surf," Lauren said. "And then I saw something like a shadow. It looked big!" What Lauren saw was a shark. It was swimming in the crest of a wave. "At first I saw only one," Lauren recalled. "And then I saw more. They were swimming together in a group."

2   Other eyewitnesses claim there were at least five sharks in the water. As soon as swimmers saw the sharks, they got out of the water fast. "I was pretty scared," Brandon Little reported with a laugh. Brandon is a local surfer who is used to seeing fish in the water. "I've just never seen that many sharks in one place!"

3   People watched with great interest as the sharks swam by. Everyone seemed to have a story to tell. Most were just glad the sharks swam away.

4   Aquarium biologist Emilio Vasquez knows a lot about sharks. "Most sharks are harmless," he told us. "The sharks the people saw are leopard sharks. They are not a threat to humans at all."

5   Vasquez explained that the sight of sharks can cause fear. "Sharks should be seen more for the amazing animals they are. It's a myth that sharks want to eat people. Sharks do much less harm to people than people do to sharks. Thousands of sharks are killed each year. Did you know that people are 250 times more likely to be killed by lightning than by a shark?

6   "Most people are afraid of sharks because of their big, razor-sharp teeth. But this doesn't mean they all eat meat. There are more than 400 species of sharks. Their diets vary quite a bit." Vasquez smiled. "People are just not on the menu."

1 Part A

What format for expository text is used in paragraph 2?

_____

_____

_____

> Reread paragraph 2. What did the swimmers do? Why? The swimmers got out of the water fast because they saw sharks. This shows a cause-and-effect relationship.

Part B

What sentence from the passage shows another example of the format from Part A?

_____

_____

_____

> Reread paragraph 5. "Vasquez explained that the sight of sharks can cause fear." Seeing sharks is the cause. Having fear is the effect.

Focus Lesson

Speeches, editorials, and advertisements are all examples of **argumentative text.** An **argument** begins with an opinion. It is meant to *persuade,* which means to convince someone to do something or respond.

You can tell when someone is using an opinion because they often use special words. These signal words might be *all, think, believe, feel, always, never, best, worst, nobody,* or *seem.*

Have you ever tried to persuade your parents to take you to see a new blockbuster movie? You probably gave your opinion of the movie and then supported that opinion with facts, examples, and reasons why you had to see it. If you were persuasive enough, your argument might have convinced your parents to take you to the movie. Many times, authors do the same thing by telling readers what they think of an idea. Then they support their opinion with facts that can be proven. They also support their argument with reasons. The **point of view** is the author's. The point of view may depend on the **author's purpose** for writing. Analyze the ideas in an argumentative text to form your own opinion. Ask yourself if there is more than one way to look at an issue. Do the author's ideas agree with what you know from your own experience? It is up to you, the reader, to determine if you believe what the author is saying.

Read this passage and answer the questions that follow.

Students Need Recess

1   Now that spring is here, everyone wants to be outside in the warm weather. But even when it's colder, students need a break from classes to exercise their bodies and give their minds a chance to think about something besides school work. Students need recess.

2   First of all, children need exercise and fresh air to be healthy. Children need at least one hour a day of exercise. If they go to after-school care, they may be stuck indoors after school. If they live in unsafe neighborhoods, they may not want to go outside to play. For some children, school is the only place they can get outside and run around.

> An author's purpose may be to inform or explain, to persuade, or to describe.
>
> *What is the author's purpose of this passage?*

3   Second, children are naturally active and need to move around during the day. But many schools have taken away recess to make more time for class work. Some schools have also stopped having physical education classes and have made lunch periods shorter. That means the students, even very young ones, could go for hours sitting at their desks. Some of them can't help wiggling or getting up from their seats. They may get in trouble for this. Children may behave better if they had recess.

> An **editorial** is an article that gives someone's opinion.
>
> *Where would you most likely see this editorial?*

4   Finally, exercise is good for the brain, as well as the body. Getting out in the fresh air gives students time away from classes. That helps them pay attention better when they go back to class. It sends oxygen to the brain to help with thinking, so students can concentrate on their work.

5   I would never say that classroom time isn't important. But students will get more out of their classes if they have recess time every day.

1 Part A

What is the main argument of the passage?

_____

_____

_____

_____

_____

> Reread the text. Look for the reasons the author gives for his point of view. In paragraph 2, the author says, "children need at least one hour a day of exercise." The author also says that children may get in trouble because they can't sit still for long periods of time and that exercise helps the brain as well as the body.

Part B

Based on the answer to Part A, what facts does the author use to support the argument?

_____

_____

_____

_____

> Reread the passage. What is the author's point of view? Think about what the author wants readers to believe. The main argument is that all students should have recess at school. Exercise is as important as class time and can help learning.

Lesson 1

Literary Text focuses on two classic stories that show how important it is to show others that you care.

 ## Lesson 2

Literary Text focuses on a poem and an adventure tale that show how important memories can be.

 ## Lesson 3

Informational Text focuses on the importance of working together, in the natural world and the musical world.

 ## Lesson 4

Informational Text focuses on how relationships can help you survive and how they can help you overcome difficulties.

Guided Practice

Read the passage and answer the questions that follow.

Matthew Insists on Puffed Sleeves

Adapted from *Anne of Green Gables*
by Lucy Maud Montgomery

See page 6
Focus Lesson:
Literary Text

1   The girls did not see Matthew, who shrank bashfully back into the shadows. He watched them shyly as they put on their caps and jackets and talked about the concert. Anne stood among them, and Matthew suddenly realized that there was something different about her. Matthew was haunted by this idea long after the girls had gone.

2   After two hours of hard thinking, Matthew knew what was different. Anne was not dressed like the other girls!

3   The more Matthew thought about it, the more he recognized that Anne never had been dressed like the other girls—not since she had come to Green Gables. His sister, Marilla, kept her clothed in plain, dark dresses, all made from the same pattern. He was sure that Anne's sleeves did not look at all like the sleeves the other girls wore. He wondered why Marilla always kept her so plainly dressed.

4   It must be all right—Marilla knew best, and Marilla was bringing her up. But surely it would do no harm to let the child have one pretty dress—something like Diana Barry always wore. Matthew decided that he would give her one. The holiday was only two weeks away, and a nice new dress would be the very thing.

5   The next evening Matthew went to Carmody to buy the dress, determined to get the worst over with. He would be at the mercy of shopkeepers when it came to buying a girl's dress.

6   Matthew decided to go to Samuel Lawson's store instead of William Blair's. The Cuthberts always went to Blair's, but Blair's daughters often waited on customers, and Matthew was in complete fear of them. Matthew must be sure of a man behind the counter, so he would go to Lawson's, where Samuel or his son would wait on him.

Guided Practice: LITERARY TEXT

7 Alas! Samuel now had a lady clerk. She was dressed with exceeding smartness and wore several bangle bracelets. Matthew was overcome with confusion.

8 "What can I do for you, Mr. Cuthbert?" Miss Lucilla Harris asked.

9 "Have you any—any—any—well now, say any garden rakes?" stammered Matthew.

10 Miss Harris looked somewhat surprised, as well she might, to hear a man ask for a garden rake in the middle of December.

11 "Anything else tonight?"

12 "Well now, I might—take—that is—look at—buy some—some hayseed."

13 "We only keep hayseed in the spring," she said.

14 "Oh, certainly—certainly," stammered Matthew, seizing the rake and making for the door. Then he remembered he had not paid for it and turned miserably back. While Miss Harris counted out his change he rallied for a final desperate attempt.

15 "Well now—if it isn't too much trouble—I might as well—that is—I'd like to look at—at—some sugar."

16 Matthew had driven halfway home before he was his own man again. He finally decided that a woman was required to cope with the situation.

© The Continental Press, Inc.
DUPLICATING THIS MATERIAL IS ILLEGAL.

UNIT 1 Relationships 33

17 Marilla was out of the question. Matthew felt sure she would throw cold water on his project at once. That left Mrs. Lynde; for of no other woman in Avonlea would Matthew have dared to ask advice. To Mrs. Lynde he went, and that good lady promptly took the matter out of the anxious man's hands.

18 "Well now, I'm much obliged," said Matthew, "and—and—I dunno—but I'd like—I think they make the sleeves different nowadays. If it wouldn't be asking too much I—I'd like them made in the new way."

19 "Puffs? Of course. You needn't worry a speck more about it, Matthew. I'll make it up in the very latest fashion," said Mrs. Lynde. When Matthew had gone, she thought, "It'll be a real satisfaction to see that poor child wearing something decent for once. But to think of Matthew taking notice of it!"

20 The morning of the holiday broke on a beautiful white world. Anne ran downstairs singing until her voice echoed through Green Gables.

21 Matthew! Isn't it a lovely holiday? I'm so glad it's white. Any other kind of holiday doesn't seem real, does it?" She stopped suddenly.

22 "Why—why—Matthew, is that for me? Oh, Matthew!"

23 Anne took the dress and looked at it in respectful silence. Oh, how pretty it was—a lovely soft brown with the gloss of silk; a skirt with dainty frills; a pintucked waist and a little lace at the neck. But the sleeves—they were the crowning glory! Long elbow cuffs, and above them two beautiful puffs!

24 "That's a present for you, Anne," said Matthew shyly. "Why—why— Anne, don't you like it? Well now—well now."

25 For Anne's eyes had suddenly filled with tears.

1 Part A

What can you tell about Matthew from the story?

_____

_____

_____

_____

> Read the story again. What do Matthew's actions and words reveal about his personality? How does he relate to women?

Part B

What two sentences from the story support your answer to Part A?

_____

_____

_____

_____

_____

_____

> Reread paragraph 1 and 2. What do you learn about Matthew?

2   Part A

How does Marilla dress Anne?

_____

_____

_____

> Read paragraphs 3 and 4 again. How are Anne's clothes different than the clothes that the other girls wear?

Part B

Why do you think Marilla dresses Anne this way?

_____

_____

_____

> You have to make an inference here based on the information in the story. How do you think Marilla herself most likely dresses?

3   Part A

Why did Matthew ask for Mrs. Lynde's help?

_____

_____

_____

_____

> Reread paragraphs 17 through 19. Think about how Matthew feels about Mrs. Lynde and how she feels about making a dress for Anne.

Part B

Judging from Anne's reaction, did she like the dress?

_____

_____

_____

_____

> Read paragraph 23 again. What does this tell you about how Anne feels about the dress?

The Boxcar Children Find a Dog

by Gertrude Chandler Warren

1   Something was moving in the woods.

2   "Keep still!" whispered Jess.

3   Benny obeyed. The three children were as motionless as stone images, huddled inside the freight car. Jess opened her mouth in order to breathe, her heart was thumping so wildly. She watched like a cat through the open door, in the direction of the rustling noise. And in a moment the trembling bushes parted, and out crawled a dog. He was an Airedale, and was pulling himself along on three legs, whimpering softly.

4   Jess drew a long breath of relief, and said to the children, "It's all right. Only a dog. But he seems to be hurt."

5   At the sound of her voice the dog lifted his eyes and wagged his tail feebly. He held up his front foot.

6   "Poor doggie," murmured Jess soothingly, as she clambered out of the car. "Let Jess see your poor lame foot." She approached the dog carefully, for she remembered that her mother had always told her never to touch a strange dog unless he wagged his tail.

7   But this dog's tail was wagging, certainly, so Jess bent over to look at the paw. An exclamation of pity escaped her when she saw it, for a stiff, sharp thorn was stuck in one of the pads of the dog's foot.

8   "I guess I can fix that," said Jess briskly. "But taking the thorn out might hurt you, old fellow."

9   The dog looked up at her as she laid his paw down, and licked her hand.

10 "Come here, Violet and Benny," directed Jess.

11 She took the animal gently in her lap and turned him on his side. She patted his head and stroked his nose with one finger, and offered him the rest of her bread crust, which she had put in her apron pocket. The dog snapped it up as if he were nearly starved. Then she held the soft paw firmly with her left hand, and pulled steadily on the thorn with her right hand. The dog did not make a sound. He lay motionless in her lap, until the thorn suddenly let go and lay in Jess' hand.

12 "Good, good!" cried Violet.

13 "Wet my handkerchief," Jess ordered briskly.

14 Violet did so, dipping it in the running brook. Jess wrapped the cool, wet folds around the hot paw, and gently squeezed it against the wound, the dog meanwhile trying to lick her hands.

15 "We'll s'prise Henry, won't we?" laughed Benny. "Now we got a dog!"

16 But you should have seen Henry stare when he got home from working!

17 "Where in the world—" began the boy.

18 "He camed to us," volunteered Benny. "He camed for a s'prise for you. And he's a nice doggie."

19 Henry knelt down to look at the visitor, who wagged his tail. "It wouldn't be a bad thing to have a watchdog," said Henry. "I worried about you all the time I was gone."

20 "Did you bring some milk?" inquired Benny, trying to be polite, but looking at the bottles with longing eyes.

21 "We'll have dinner right away," said Jess.

22 "And then tomorrow we'll start having three meals every day," laughed Jess.

23 The brown loaf was cut into five thick squares and the cheese into four.

24 "Dogs don't eat cheese," Benny remarked cheerfully. The poor little fellow was glad of it, too, for he was very hungry. He could hardly wait for Jess to set the milk bottles in the center of the table and heap the blueberries in four little mounds, one at each place.

25 "I'm sorry we haven't cups," Jess remarked. "We'll just have to drink out of the same bottle."

26 "No, we won't," said Henry. "We'll drink half of each bottle, so that will make at least two things to drink out of."

27 "We are going to sleep on beds tonight, and just as soon as we get our beds made, we are all going to be washed," said Jess. She was covering the last two soft beds with the two aprons. Then, armed with the big cake of soap, she led the way to the brook.

28 The dog watched them anxiously, but when Jess said, "Lie still," he obeyed. From the moment Jess drew the thorn from his foot he was her dog, to obey her slightest command and to follow her wherever she went.

1 Part A

What is the main idea of this story?

A The children find a hungry dog and feed him.

B The children find a dog and decide to keep him.

C Benny is happy that they now have milk to drink.

D After work, Henry brings the children cheese to eat.

Part B

Which sentence from the story best supports the answer to Part A?

A "The dog snapped it up as if he were nearly starved."

B "'Dogs don't eat cheese,' Benny remarked cheerfully."

C "'It wouldn't be a bad thing to have a watchdog,' said Henry."

D "She took the animal gently in her lap and turned him on his side."

2 Part A

Who does the dog like best?

A Jess

B Benny

C Henry

D Violet

Part B

What did this character do that made the dog like him or her?

A trained him to lie still

B fed him bread and cheese

C took a thorn out of his paw

D petted him for wagging his tail

3 Part A

Using details from the story, which of the four children is most likely the youngest?

A Jess

B Benny

C Henry

D Violet

Part B

Which line from the text helps most in deciding the answer to Part A?

A "'He camed for a s'prise for you. And he's a nice doggie.'"

B "'But taking the thorn out might hurt you, old fellow.'"

C "'Dogs don't eat cheese,' Benny remarked cheerfully."

D "The poor little fellow was glad of it, too, for he was very hungry."

Guided Practice

Read the poem and answer the questions that follow.

Grandmother's Quilt

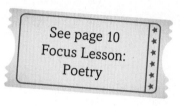

See page 10
Focus Lesson:
Poetry

1 Why, yes, dear, we can put it by. It does seem out of place
On top of these down comforts and this spread of silk and lace,
You see, I'm used to having it lie so, across my feet,
But maybe I won't need it here, with this nice furnace heat.

2 I made it? Yes, dear, long ago. 'Twas lots of work, you think?
Oh, not so much. My rose quilt, now, all white and green and pink,
Is really handsome. This is just a plain, log cabin block,
Pieced out of odds and ends; but still—now that's your papa's frock
Before he walked, and this bit here is his first little suit.
I trimmed it up with silver braid. My, but he did look cute!

3 That red there in the centers, was your Aunt Ruth's for her name,
Her grandmother made all her clothes, before the others came.
Those plaids? The younger girls', they were. I dressed them just alike.
And this was baby Winnie's sack—the precious little tyke!
Ma wore this gown to visit me (they drove the whole way then).
And little Edson wore this waist. He never came again.

4 This lavender par'matta was your great-aunt Jane's—poor dear!
Mine was a sprig, with the lilac ground; see, in the corner here.
Such goods were high in war times. Ah, that scrap of army blue;
Your bright eyes spied it! Yes, dear child, that has its memories, too.
They sent him home on furlough once—our soldier brother Ned;
But somewhere, now, the dear boy sleeps among the unknown dead.

5 That flowered patch? Well, now, to think you'd pick that from the rest!
Why, dearie—yes, it's satin ribbed—that's grandpa's wedding vest!
Just odds and ends! Not great for looks. My rose quilt's nicer, far,
Or the redwork basket pattern, or the double-pointed star.
But, somehow—What! We'll leave it here? The bed won't look so neat,
But I think I would sleep better with it so, across my feet.

1 Part A

Who is the narrator of this poem?

_____

_____

_____

> The narrator is the speaker in a poem. It can be someone in or outside the poem. Who is the speaker of this poem?

Part B

What two lines in the poem support your answer to Part A?

_____

_____

_____

_____

_____

> Reread the first stanza. The speaker uses the pronoun _I_. The title of the poem is also a clue.

2 Part A

What is the theme of the poem?

_____

_____

_____

_____

_____

> The theme of a poem, or a story, is the message the author is trying to convey. What is the speaker of this poem trying to say?

Part B

Which line or lines in the poem support the theme?

_____

_____

_____

_____

> Read the poem again. Many lines in the poem support the theme. You need to choose only one idea.

3   Part A

Read this line from the first stanza of the poem.

> "'Why, yes, dear, we can put it by.'"

What does the word *by* mean as it is used here?

_____

_____

_____

> Read the next line of the poem. Often, neighboring words and lines reveal clues about a word's meaning.

Part B

Which line in the poem helped you answer the question in Part A?

_____

_____

_____

_____

_____

> Think about what the speaker says in the first stanza. Find a part of the poem that helped you determine the meaning of the word *by.* Look for context clues.

The Pirates Feast and Plot

Adapted from *Treasure Island*
by *Robert Louis Stevenson*

Young Jim Hawkins is being held by Long John Silver and the other pirates on the island. Jim is pretending to work with the pirates until he can escape and find his friends. Captain Flint is Silver's parrot.

1   "Jim," said Silver when we were alone, "if I saved your life, you saved mine; and I'll not forget it. I seen the doctor waving you to run for it—with the tail of my eye, I did; and I seen you say no, as plain as hearing. Jim, that's one to you. This is the first glint of hope I had since the attack failed, and I owe it you. And now, Jim, we're to go in for this here treasure-hunting, with sealed orders too, and I don't like it; and you and me must stick close, back to back like, and we'll save our necks in spite o' fate and fortune."

2   Just then a man hailed us from the fire that breakfast was ready, and we were soon seated here and there about the sand over biscuit and fried salt pork. They had lit a fire fit to roast an ox, and it was now grown so hot that they could only approach it from the windward, and even there not without precaution. In the same wasteful spirit, they had cooked, I suppose, three times more than we could eat. One of them, with an empty laugh, threw what was left into the fire, which blazed and roared again over this unusual fuel. I never in my life saw men so careless of the future; hand to mouth is the only word that can describe their way of doing.

3   Even Silver, eating away, with Captain Flint perched upon his shoulder, had not a word of blame for their recklessness. And this surprised me, for I thought he had never shown himself so clever as he did then.

4   "Aye, mates," said he, "it's lucky you have Barbecue to think for you with this here head. I got what I wanted, I did. Sure enough, they have the ship. Where they have it, I don't know yet; but once we hit the treasure, we'll have

to jump about and find out. And then, mates, us that has the boats, I reckon, has the upper hand."

5   Thus he kept running on, with his mouth full of the hot bacon; thus he restored their hope and confidence, and, I more than suspect, repaired his own at the same time.

6   "As for hostage," he continued, "that's his last talk, I guess, with them he loves so dear. I've got my piece o' news, and thanky to him for that; but it's over and done. I'll take him in a line when we go treasure-hunting, for we'll keep him like so much gold, in case of accidents, you mark, and in the meantime. Once we got the ship and treasure both and off to sea like jolly companions, why then we'll talk Mr. Hawkins over, we will, and we'll give him his share, to be sure, for all his kindness."

7   It was no wonder the men were in a good mood now. For my part, I was horribly cast down. Should the scheme he had now sketched prove possible, Silver, already doubly a traitor, would not hesitate to follow it. He had still a foot in either camp.

1   Part A

What can you tell about the pirates from paragraph 2?

A   They are friendly.

B   They are determined.

C   They are not intelligent.

D   They are not responsible.

Part B

Which phrase from paragraph 2 best supports the answer to Part A?

A   "about in the sand"

B   "careless of the future"

C   "hailed us from the fire"

D   "over biscuit and fried pork"

UNIT 1 Relationships   47

2 Part A

How is Jim different from Silver?

A   He is kind.

B   He is clever.

C   He is greedy.

D   He is grateful.

Part B

What does Jim do that supports the answer in Part A?

A   He tricks Silver.

B   He stays with Silver.

C   He thanks the pirates.

D   He hunts for the treasure.

3 Part A

What is the universal theme of the story?

A   good versus evil

B   person versus nature

C   love and friendship

D   service and sacrifice

Part B

Based on your answer to Part A, which best shows the universal theme?

A   Jim is caring, but Silver is not.

B   Jim knows Silver will reward him.

C   The pirates know each other well.

D   The pirates may be burned by the fire.

Guided Practice

Read the passage and answer the questions that follow.

A Sweet Relationship

See page 25
Focus Lesson:
Expository Text

1 People have been eating honey for thousands of years. Honey has even been found in the Ancient Egyptian pyramids. Many people enjoy having honey on toast or in tea. However, they may not think much about how the honey gets to the grocery stores where they buy it. Many times beekeepers help care for and protect the hives so the bees can stay busy making honey.

2 The National Honey Board estimates that 211,600 beekeepers in the United States tend some three million honey-producing colonies. The average worker bee makes only one-twelfth of a teaspoon in its lifetime. Bees visit 50 to 100 flowers during one collection trip, tapping two million flowers to produce one pound of honey. Americans on average eat about one pound of honey a year. A tablespoon of honey contains calcium, potassium, and small amounts of other minerals and vitamins. Scientists have found other benefits of eating honey, too.

3 A worker bee's life revolves around pleasing a queen bee, which lives about 50 times longer than a worker bee. Therefore, beekeepers and the industry invest a great deal of time and effort into making queen bees. To produce queen bees, beekeepers take a worker bee egg and seal it into a

cell cup. The hive needs a queen, so the worker bees pay special attention to the egg in the cell cup. They feed it special food to help it grow big and strong. Only the queen bee lays all the eggs to add workers to the colony.

A Family Business

4   Dale Bauer owns a honey business near Fertile, Minnesota. In 1951, then 16-year-old Bauer needed a job and went to work for a local beekeeper. After a few years of military service, the Nebraska native and his wife, Lois, moved to her neck of the woods in northwestern Minnesota. Beekeeping seemed as good a job as any other, so the couple began producing honey.

5   The bees and hives produce the most honey around the last week of June in northern Minnesota. From then until the first frosts, the Bauer family is busy. The sealed honeycombs are collected and the wax is cut. Special machines spin the combs to separate the wax from the honey. Beekeepers collect one pound of wax for every 100 pounds of honey. The wax is sold so it can be made into candles or floor wax and cosmetics. At the Bauers' operation, the honey is loaded into 50,000-pound tankers and shipped to the Sioux City plant. Two to three tankers leave the family operation every week.

6   After unloading at the plant, the honey is melted to make it easier to pour and process. The honey is first filtered, and then put into bottles and jars. Soon these packages of honey are shipped to stores all across the country where shoppers buy them. The honey may end up in a cup of tea or may be used in recipes.

Honey Lemon Chicken

Ingredients

- 1 tablespoon vegetable oil
- 4 pounds chicken (cut into 8 pieces)
- $\frac{1}{2}$ cup all-purpose flour
- 1 teaspoon salt
- $\frac{1}{4}$ cup honey
- $\frac{1}{4}$ cup lemon juice

Directions

1. Preheat oven to 375 degrees. Line a baking pan with foil for easy cleanup. Lightly oil the foil.

2. Combine flour and salt in a plastic bag. Shake chicken pieces in flour mixture, remove from bag, and place on prepared pan.

3. Bake for 45 minutes.

4. Combine honey and lemon. Spoon mixture over chicken to glaze chicken pieces. Bake another 15 minutes. Juices should run clear when pierced with a fork. Serves 8.

Nutritional Information per serving	
Calories: 330	Protein: 6g
Total fat: 8g	Calcium: 2%
Cholesterol: 150mg	Vitamin A: 2%
Sodium: 160mg	Vitamin C: 15%
Dietary fiber: 0 g	Iron: 15%
Carbohydrates: 15g	

Source: USDA/Montana State University Extension Service

1   **Part A**

How is the section "A Family Business" organized?

_____

_____

_____

_____

> Read this section again. Notice that Dale Bauer is 16 years old in the beginning of the section. How old is he at the end of the section?

Part B

Which paragraph in the first half of the article has the same organization as "A Family Business"?

_____

_____

_____

_____

> The first paragraph is an introduction, so look closely at paragraphs 2 and 3. What do the paragraphs tell about?

2   Part A

What is the main idea of the article?

_____

_____

_____

> Reread the article. Think about what it is mostly about. Reread the title. It offers a clue.

Part B

Which sentence in the article supports the answer to Part A?

_____

_____

_____

_____

_____

> Reread paragraph 1. Look for a sentence that expresses the same idea as your answer to Part A.

3 Part A

Why did the author include paragraph 5?

_____

_____

_____

_____

> Reread paragraph 5. What kind of information does it provide? What does it tell about the Bauer family?

Part B

What is the purpose of paragraph 6?

_____

_____

_____

_____

> Reread paragraph 5. How does it lead into paragraph 6? Think about why paragraph 6 is important to the article.

4   Part A

Why do you think the author included the recipe?

_____

_____

_____

> Think about what ingredients are in the recipe. How might the recipe be related to the passage?

Part B

How are the passage and the recipe alike?

_____

_____

_____

> Reread the recipe. What do the passage and the recipe have in common?

Read the passage and answer the questions that follow.

A Magical Partnership

by DeShawn Jackson

1   John Lennon and Paul McCartney's partnership is one of the most famous in the history of music. John and Paul met in 1957 when they were just teenagers. At 15, Paul already had his head full of music. John started his own band, the Quarrymen, when he was 16. When Paul went to hear the Quarrymen play near Liverpool, England, he stayed afterward to meet John Lennon.

2   When Paul picked up a guitar and played, John could see that he was incredibly talented. John wanted to ask him to join the band, but he was concerned that Paul would want to be the leader. John wanted to remain the leader. He liked it when people did what he said. However, Paul was as smart and as strong as John was, and they watched each other closely at that first meeting. They were interested in playing together, but they were being careful. One friend later said they circled each other like cats.

3   John described his choice this way: "I had a group. I was the singer and the leader; then I met Paul, and I had to make a decision: Was it better to have a guy who was better than the guy I had in? To make the group stronger, or to let me be stronger?" He decided that he wanted to work with Paul, but this would not always be easy.

4   John's group became the Beatles, one of the most famous rock bands in history. Between 1962 and 1970, the Beatles had 15 number-one hit songs. The band has sold more than 3.3 billion albums (yes, *billion*) and their albums still sell today.

5   During their years together, John and Paul wrote more than 150 songs. From the start, they credited all their songs to Lennon/McCartney, even if one had done most of the writing on his own. Unlike some songwriting teams, they both wrote music and words. They encouraged each other and wrote better together than alone. Their early hits included "Please Please Me," "I Want To Hold Your Hand," and "She Loves You." However, sometimes their friendship was more like a competition. "I would bring in a song and you could sort of see John stiffen a bit," Paul said. "Next day he'd bring in a song and I'd sort of stiffen. And it was like, 'Oh, you're going to do that, are you? Right. You wait till I come up with something tomorrow.'" John remained the leader of the band for several years, but Paul was more likely to interact with the audience, which made some fans believe he was the leader.

6   The band quickly gained worldwide fame. Lennon/McCartney songs amazed fans and influenced other bands. Songs such as "Yesterday" and "Ticket to Ride" became number-one hits while albums *Sgt. Pepper's Lonely Hearts Club Band*, *Revolver*, and *Rubber Soul* topped the album charts. The Beatles provided fresh, new songs that reflected the social changes of the 1960s. The combination of the brilliant songwriters and the thrilling band made it seem like the magic would never end.

7   Like all good things, however, the magic did end. The Beatles stopped touring because their adoring fans made so much noise that their music could not be heard. The years of forced closeness had become smothering, and John and Paul were choosing new paths, away from the band and each other. The Beatles made three more number-one albums—*Abbey Road*, *The Beatles* (the White Album), and *Let It Be.* Then they called it quits.

8   Disagreements about who was the leader had continued until the end. In spite of the breakup, however, the bond shared by John and Paul wasn't completely broken. And, most important, the astonishing catalog of music the Lennon/McCartney partnership produced remains popular and influential, even many years later.

1   Part A

What difficult decision did John Lennon have to make in 1957?

A   whether to write songs on his own or find a partner

B   whether to stay with his group or go out on his own

C   whether to write upbeat songs or songs with messages

D   whether to make his group stronger or himself stronger

Part B

Based on the answer to Part A, how did John resolve his problem?

A   He asked Paul McCartney to join his band.

B   He decided to find a partner to write songs with.

C   He asked Paul McCartney to write upbeat songs.

D   He decided to make himself a stronger band leader.

2   Part A

Which words best describe John and Paul's working relationship?

A   honest but polite

B   special but difficult

C   dangerous and foolish

D   comfortable and friendly

Part B

Which paragraph from the article best supports the answer to Part A?

A   paragraph 3

B   paragraph 5

C   paragraph 7

D   paragraph 8

3 **Part A**

What is the main idea of the article?

A   John and Paul had a very successful rock band.

B   John and Paul struggled to get along for many years.

C   The music of John and Paul is still popular after many years.

D   Their different styles helped John and Paul write better songs.

Part B

Which sentence from the article best supports the answer to Part A?

A   "They encouraged each other and wrote better together than alone."

B   "They were interested in playing together, but they were being careful."

C   "Disagreements about who was the leader had continued until the end."

D   "John's group became the Beatles, one of the most famous rock bands in history."

Guided Practice

Read the passage and answer the questions that follow.

See page 25
Focus Lesson:
Expository Text

Military Therapy Dogs Put Soldiers at Ease

1   FORT LEWIS, WASH. — The 98th Medical Combat Stress Control Detachment, a unit of about 50 soldiers and officers, has succeeded on many missions. The enemy that the unit fights is stress, and the soldiers' best weapons are therapy dogs.

2   Butch and Zack received challenging training by America's VetDogs, a nonprofit organization that raises and donates dogs to military units and veterans with needs. The dogs continued their training alongside their military partners as they prepared for their assignments.

3   Commander of 98th Med. Det. and psychiatric nurse practitioner, Lt. Col. John Gourley, said the unit spent one week training with four dogs before selecting Butch and Zack because of their nature.

4   "Butch and Zack are more outgoing and they're more engaging with people," Gourley said. "What we need the dogs to be able to do is break the ice with the soldiers."

5   Breaking the ice can be an important first step in getting a soldier help. A dozen providers, including psychiatrists, psychologists, psychiatric nurse practitioners, social workers, and occupational therapists, travel with the detachment. They split into many small units to provide treatment at many places. Their main challenge is getting soldiers into their clinics for care. That's where the dogs help the most.

6   Butch, a 23-month-old black Labrador retriever, proved her value with each soldier she met as she made her way around a JBLM training site. Walking the grounds with her new handler, Spc. Jon Miles, the pair was received with open arms at every stop.

7   "There's really no real rhyme or exact reason why, but it works," Miles said of soldiers' fondness for Butch as they flocked to pet her.

8   Miles remembered a previous assignment without the bonus of therapy dogs. Instead, he and fellow soldiers adopted and cared for several local dogs in the area.

9   "Dogs generally have a calming effect on people, so if soldiers are having a hard time because they're homesick or stressed out at work," the therapy dogs and trainers can help them calm down, he said. "It's an opening for them to relax and speak with us so we can see if they need help."

10   For Sgt. Liz Wright, a mechanic with 3rd Brigade, 2nd Infantry Division, seeing Butch broke up the boredom of a long day working outside in the cold.

11   "We had been here all day working hard, putting up tents, then we saw them," Wright said. "We stopped what we were doing and went over to pet her. It took our minds off what we were doing out in the cold."

12   Gourley expects other troops will have similar reactions. Not everyone who comes in contact with Butch or Zack will be referred to a clinic or need help of any kind. Simply playing with the dogs can be enough to make them happier.

13   "Often times a big tough guy (who) doesn't want to talk to a mental health person will feel comfortable getting down and talking while petting the dog," Gourley said.

1 Part A

What is the main idea of the article?

_____

_____

_____

> Reread the article. What is it mostly about?

Part B

What effect did the dogs have on soldiers discussed in the article?

_____

_____

_____

_____

> Reread the article. Look for people describing how people react to the dogs. How does this support the main idea?

2 Part A

Why are the dogs traveling with mental-health teams?

_____

_____

_____

> Reread the article. What are the mental-health teams hoping to do?

Part B

Where does this article explain the answer to Part A?

_____

_____

_____

> Reread the information about the teams. What does it say about the dogs?

3   Part A

In paragraph 4, what does Gourley mean by "break the ice"?

_____

_____

_____

_____

_____

> Reread the paragraph. What information before and after the words helps explain the meaning?

Part B

How does breaking the ice help the mental-health teams?

_____

_____

_____

_____

> Think about what the dogs do to help the people on the teams.

Sponges Play Host to Many Guests

by Nikki Baumann

1   A sponge is an organism that lives in the ocean. It attaches itself to an object on the ocean floor, such as a rock, and remains there for the rest of its life. A sponge may have a great deal of company in its ocean-floor home. It might live near other sponges and even have a few visitors and residents within it.

2   Ocean sponges are similar to the kitchen sponges you might find in your house. Sponges are porous, which means that they consist of many tiny holes. These holes might be little tunnels or long tubes. Many organisms in need of shelter are small enough to hide inside these holes in ocean sponges. The organism gets shelter from the sponge, but doesn't harm the sponge. This arrangement, in which only one organism benefits, is called a *commensal relationship.* Scientists have found many kinds of creatures, including shrimp and worms, living in sponges. Some large sponges are called living hotels, because hundreds of creatures live inside them.

Life in a Sponge

3   Sponges make good homes for small ocean organisms for several reasons. In addition to giving these little creatures shelter, sponges supply food. Sponges don't move around or catch food, but they suck in water that contains food. This water flows through the sponge's body, through all the little chambers and tunnels, while the sponge filters the food from the water. Anything living inside the sponge has access to the food the sponge has removed from the water. The word *commensalism* literally means, "eating from the same table." You can see why a sponge is an excellent choice as a host for a commensal organism.

4   Sometimes many different kinds of organisms live within a sponge. These organisms are called *endocommensal* species, and they form a community within the sponge. The size and shape of this community depends on the size and shape of the sponge. Some different types of organisms living within a sponge work together to make sure the community survives. For example, they take turns caring for each other's young. So, life within a sponge is more than comfortable living space and an endless supply of food. Residents have the possibility of a social life as well!

5   Scientists know a great deal about sponges, but they also have much more to learn. They have discovered more than 7,000 species of sponges on the ocean floor, but they believe that there are probably thousands more species yet to be discovered.

1   Part A

Read this sentence from the passage.

"This water flows through the sponge's body, through all the little chambers and tunnels, while the sponge filters the food from the water."

What does the word *filters* mean?

A   cleans

B   creates

C   discovers

D   separates

Part B

Which sentence helped you determine the answer to Part A?

A   "The word *commensalism* literally means, 'eating from the same table.'"

B   "In addition to giving these little creatures shelter, sponges supply food."

C   "Anything living inside the sponge has access to the food the sponge has removed from the water."

D   "Sponges don't move around or catch food, but they suck in water that contains food."

2 Part A

How does the picture contribute to your understanding of sponges?

A   It shows what a sponge will attach itself to.

B   It shows what the holes in a sponge look like.

C   It shows that there are many different types of sponges.

D   It shows what the organisms that live in a sponge look like.

Part B

Which paragraph most closely relates to the answer to Part A?

A   paragraph 1

B   paragraph 2

C   paragraph 4

D   paragraph 5

3 Part A

What is the main idea of the article?

A   Ocean sponges are just like kitchen sponges.

B   Sponges make good homes for other creatures.

C   Scientists continue to learn about ocean sponges.

D   Sponges are organisms that live on the ocean floor.

Part B

What sentence best supports the answer to Part A?

A   "Commensal relationships don't hurt the host animal."

B   "Some organisms living within a sponge help one another."

C   "Sponges firmly attach themselves to the ocean floor for life."

D   "Sponges provide shelter and bring in food for other organisms."

Lesson 1

Literary Text shows the importance of determination through characters in a play and a folktale.

 ## Lesson 2

Literary Text focuses on how determination in solving a problem is rewarded in two fiction stories.

 ## Lesson 3

Informational Text focuses on what happens when you are determined to achieve a goal.

 ## Lesson 4

Informational Text focuses on what happens when creativity is used in the kitchen and how animals adapt in a frozen world.

Guided Practice

Read the play and answer the questions that follow.

The Wise Crow

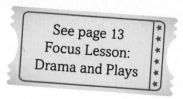

See page 13
Focus Lesson:
Drama and Plays

Cast of Characters

Crow

Sparrow

On a summer day, Crow and Sparrow meet at a spring in a meadow.
A pitcher sits on a low stone wall near the spring.

Sparrow: Ah me, the spring is dry!

Crow: All the springs are dry!

Sparrow: There may be water in the brook.

Crow: No, the brook is dry.

Sparrow: What shall we do? My throat is so dry, I cannot sing. I croak like a crow instead.

Crow: *(frowning first at Sparrow, and then at the pitcher on the stone wall)* There may be water in this pitcher. I will see. Aha! Here is water! Come and drink.

Sparrow: I cannot reach it. It is too low.

Crow: Stretch your neck!

Sparrow: I stretch and stretch—I cannot reach it.

Crow: Why, neither can I! Stretch as I will, I cannot reach it.

Sparrow: What shall we do?

Crow: We will break the pitcher. Come, now!

Sparrow: I strike and strike.

Crow: I strike and strike, too. I hit it harder and harder.

Sparrow: We cannot break it.

Crow: No, you are right, we cannot break it.

Sparrow: What shall we do?

Crow: Let us try to overturn it. Come, now!

Sparrow: I push and push.

Crow: I push and push. I am larger and taller, but the pitcher is very heavy.

Sparrow: We cannot overturn it.

Crow: No, we cannot overturn it, and now we are hotter than ever. I am even more thirsty than I was before.

Sparrow: We must have water! What shall we do?

Crow: My uncle said, "Where there is a will there is a way." Let me think. Ah, I know the way to get the water!

She drops pebbles into the pitcher.

Sparrow: Why do you drop pebbles in the pitcher?

Crow drops in more pebbles; the water rises. Sparrow hops around as he watches.

Sparrow: Please tell me why you do that! I am very curious to know what you are doing!

Crow: Now come and drink, Mister Sparrow!

Sparrow: *(taking a sip)* Why, I can reach the water! How strange! How very strange! Crow, you are very wise and clever! Now that I have had a drink, I can sing again!

1 Part A

What is the problem that Sparrow and Crow have?

_____

_____

_____

_____

_____

> Reread the beginning of the play. Sparrow and Crow are looking for something they need. What is it?

Part B

Based on your answer to Part A, how do Sparrow and Crow solve the problem?

_____

_____

_____

_____

_____

> Think about what Sparrow and Crow do. What do they do to get what they need?

2   Part A

If this play were written as a short story, what would it have that it does not have now?

_____

_____

_____

_____

A short story looks and reads differently than a play. How are they different?

Part B

Based on your answer to Part A, if this play were written as a short story, what would it not have that it has now?

_____

_____

_____

_____

_____

What would be taken out if this play were rewritten as a short story?

3 **Part A**

What is the theme of this play?

_____

_____

_____

_____

_____

> The theme is the lesson that the play teaches. Think about the story and what happens. What is the lesson it teaches?

Part B

Does the theme describe Sparrow's behavior in the play?

_____

_____

_____

_____

_____

> Think about what Sparrow does in the play. Does Sparrow help solve the problem? Or, does Crow solve the problem on her own? What would Sparrow have done if Crow had not been there?

Read the passage and answer the questions that follow.

Heron and Hummingbird

a Native American tale

1   Long ago, when animals ruled the world, Heron and Hummingbird were best friends. They both loved to eat fish. Hummingbird liked to eat tiny minnows, but Heron preferred to eat bigger fish.

2   One day Hummingbird said, "Heron, I am afraid there are not enough fish in the rivers and lakes for both of us. Someday there might not be any fish left, so let's have a race. The winner of the race shall have all the fish in the world."

3   Heron agreed to the race. The friends determined the race would last for four days. The winner of the race would be the first one to sit at the top of the old dead tree at the farthest bend in the river.

4   The next morning, just as the sun peeked over the horizon, the race started. Hummingbird flew several times around Heron, before flying away swiftly and leaving Heron far behind. Heron continued flying steadily forward. Hummingbird was fast, but was easily distracted by all the pretty flowers along the way. Hummingbird would stop to investigate and sip the sweet nectar from the flowers.

5   Meanwhile, Heron continued flying steadily forward. Around noon on the first day, Heron caught up to Hummingbird. While Hummingbird sipped sweet nectar, Heron became the leader of the race. When Hummingbird realized that Heron had taken the lead, Hummingbird hurried to reach Heron. By late afternoon, Hummingbird had caught up with Heron. Hummingbird flew several times around Heron, before flying away swiftly and leaving Heron far behind.

6   Hummingbird decided to stop and rest for the night because she was exhausted from flying so quickly. Just as the sun dipped below the horizon, Hummingbird found a nice, comfortable place to perch and sleep all night long. Meanwhile, Heron continued flying steadily forward throughout the night.

7   On the morning of the second day, Hummingbird woke rested and refreshed. Remembering the race, Hummingbird flew off in a hurry to reach Heron. Around noon, Hummingbird caught up with Heron. Hummingbird

flew several times around Heron before flying away swiftly and leaving Heron far behind. Again, Hummingbird became distracted by the pretty flowers. He flew off to investigate and sip their sweet nectar.

8   Once again, Heron continued flying steadily forward. And so it went for the rest of the race. Hummingbird quickly passed Heron until the pretty flowers caught Hummingbird's attention. Hummingbird would stop to investigate and sip the sweet nectar from the flowers. Heron would continue flying steadily forward. Each night Hummingbird would rest while Heron would fly on.

9   Hummingbird woke on the morning of the fourth day rested and refreshed. Remembering the race, Hummingbird quickly flew off. The far bend in the river was becoming visible and Hummingbird was sure of victory. When Hummingbird rounded the bend, there was Heron sitting at the very top of the old dead tree. Heron had won the race by flying steadily forward while Hummingbird was distracted or resting.

10   From that day on, Heron fished all the rivers and lakes, while Hummingbird sipped sweet nectar from flowers like those discovered during the race.

1   Part A

What does Hummingbird do that keeps him from winning the race?

A   eats fish

B   sips nectar

C   stops to rest

D   flies in circles

Part B

Based on your answer to Part A, why isn't Hummingbird worried about losing the race because of this?

A   He can fly very fast.

B   He flies steadily forward.

C   He thinks he is very smart.

D   He knows Heron will stop to rest.

2 **Part A**

Which word best describes Heron?

A tricky

B truthful

C faithful

D pleasant

Part B

Which sentence from the passage best supports the answer to Part A?

A "Once again, Heron continued flying steadily forward."

B "By late afternoon, Hummingbird had caught up with Heron."

C "When Hummingbird rounded the bend, there was Heron sitting at the very top of the old dead tree."

D "Hummingbird flew several times around Heron, before flying away swiftly and leaving Heron far behind."

3 **Part A**

What is the theme of this story?

A Good friends should not race against each other.

B The bird that flies the fastest should win the race.

C Flying slow and steady might help a bird win a race.

D A heron should not win a race against a hummingbird.

Part B

Which sentence best supports the theme?

A Hummingbird wants to race against Heron.

B Hummingbird flies much faster than Heron.

C Heron wins the race against Hummingbird.

D Heron agrees to race Hummingbird for four days.

Guided Practice

Read the passage and answer the questions that follow.

Roughing It

by Savonna Malik

See page 6
Focus Lesson:
Literary Text

1   Serena and Kanesha struggled to lift the heavy tent. The poles were very long, but bent easily. They had to lift the middle of the pole, the part that held up the tent roof, so they could put the ends into little pockets on the tent corners.

2   "It's almost up, Kanesha! Keep lifting!" Serena shouted. "The first pole is always the hardest!" She slipped her end of the pole into its little pocket and held the slim pole steady.

3   "I got it!" Kanesha called back, grinning. She had never helped set up a tent before. The friends bent the ends of the second pole, making it a perfect match to the first one, and quickly tucked the ends into the pockets. They hammered a few tent stakes into the ground to keep the tent from blowing away and stood back to admire their work. They checked inside to see how it looked. It was a little dark, so Kanesha switched on the small battery lantern they had brought along.

4   "There's nothing better than a night under the stars," called Kanesha's father from the back porch. The girls grinned. As long as they didn't look at the house behind them—and Mr. Barnett's grill—they could pretend they were out in the woods, cooking food over an open fire. Right now, though, the delicious smell of grilled chicken was beckoning them. They quickly unrolled their sleeping bags in the tent, tossed pillows inside, and raced to the table.

5   The girls feasted on corn and chicken. After dinner they toasted marshmallows over the coals. Kanesha liked hers just melted and golden brown on all sides, but Serena liked dark and crispy marshmallows. They pressed the sweet melted gobs between chocolate bits and graham crackers. Serena bit heartily into the dessert, and then licked chocolate and marshmallows from her fingers.

6   Later, in the twilight, Serena and Kanesha chased fireflies across the yard. As darkness began to fall, Kanesha was glad she had left the lantern glowing inside the tent. It looked homey and welcoming as they walked toward it. Smiling, the girls crept into their cozy overnight home.

7   "EEEWW!" shrieked Kanesha, diving out of the tent. Feathery wings brushed across Serena's face. Something buzzed at her ear. She quickly followed her friend through the tent flap and up to the back porch.

8   "We left the light on and the tent flap unzipped," Serena said sadly. "All the bugs got in." Serena knew Kanesha didn't like bugs. What if their camping trip was over? Then she saw a broom leaning against the house. She saw Mr. Barnett's newspaper on a chair.

9   "Wait, Kanesha—just calm down, okay? I have an idea," Serena said. She grabbed the broom and newspaper, straightened her shoulders, and slipped back into the tent. Serena worked hard. She used the newspaper to chase the flying insects out of the tent. She used the broom to sweep away anything crawling on the floor. Kanesha calmed down and helped to shake out the sleeping bags and pillows. The friends crawled back into the tent, zipped the flap closed, and spread out their sleeping bags. Finally, they turned out the light.

10   "There's nothing better than a night under the stars," Serena giggled.

11   "Yes, there is!" said Kanesha. "It's a *bug-free* night under the stars!"

1   Part A

What two mistakes did the girls make after they set up their camp?

_____

_____

_____

> Think about what the girls did. Serena names these mistakes toward the end of the story.

Part B

Based on your answer to Part A, what happened because of these mistakes?

_____

_____

_____

> What caused Kanesha to shriek?

2 Part A

How does Serena feel about bugs?

_____

_____

_____

> Think about what Serena does. What did she do when the bugs flew around her head?

Part B

Based on the answer to Part A, what did Serena do?

_____

_____

_____

> Reread the last few paragraphs of the story. How did Serena react?

3   Part A

Write a sentence or sentences that summarize the story.

_____

_____

_____

_____

_____

> A summary gives the most important points of a text. Think about the important events in the story.

Part B

What sentence supports your answer in Part A?

_____

_____

> Reread paragraph 8. Look for a sentence that supports a point you made in your summary. Think about causes and their effects.

My Father and the Baby Dragon

by Ruth Stiles Gannett

1   My father, who was just a boy then, walked back and forth, trying to think of some way to cross the river. He found a high flagpole with a rope going over to the other side. The rope went through a loop at the top of the pole and then down the pole and around a large crank. A sign on the crank said:

TO SUMMON DRAGON, YANK THE CRANK
REPORT DISORDERLY CONDUCT TO GORILLA

2   From what the cat had told my father, he knew that the other end of the rope was tied around the dragon's neck, and he felt sorrier than ever. What a life for a baby dragon!

3   My father knew that if he called to the dragon, the gorilla would surely hear him. He thought about climbing the pole and going across on the rope. But the river was very muddy, and all sorts of unfriendly things might live in it. Then he heard a loud splash behind him.

4   "It's me, Crocodile," said a voice. "The water's lovely, and I have a craving for something sweet. Won't you come in for a swim?"

5   "Oh, no thank you," said my father. "I never swim after sundown. But perhaps you'd like a lollipop? Perhaps you have friends who would like lollipops, too?"

6   "Lollipops!" said the crocodile. "Why, that is a treat! How about it, boys?"

7   A chorus of voices shouted, "Lollipops!" My father counted 17 crocodiles with their heads peeping out of the water.

8   "That's fine," said my father. He got out 17 pink lollipops and rubber bands. "I'll stick one here in the bank for you," he said to the first crocodile.

9   The crocodile swam up and tasted it. "Delicious!" he said.

10   "Now," said my father, "I'll just walk along your back and fasten another lollipop to the tip of your tail with a rubber band. You don't mind, do you?"

11   "Oh no, not in the least," said the crocodile. My father ran along his back and fastened the lollipop with a rubber band.

12   "Who's next?" said my father, and a second crocodile swam up and began licking that lollipop.

13   "Now, you gentlemen can save a lot of time if you just line up across the river," said my father, "and I'll be along to give you each a lollipop."

14   So the crocodiles lined up right across the river with their tails in the air, waiting for my father to fasten on the rest of the lollipops. The tail of the 17th crocodile touched the other bank.

15   Just as my father was crossing the back of the fifteenth crocodile, the noise of the monkeys suddenly stopped. Then he could hear seven furious tigers and one raging rhinoceros and two seething lions and one ranting gorilla all yelling, "It's a trick! It's a trick! He must be after our dragon. Get him!" The whole crowd stampeded down to the bank. My father didn't have a moment to spare.

16   By now the dragon realized that my father was coming to rescue him. He ran out of the bushes and jumped up and down yelling. "Here I am! I'm right here! Hurry, the others are coming over on the crocodiles, too."

17   My father ran up to the dragon and took out his jackknife. "Steady, old boy. We'll make it. Just stand still," he told the dragon as he began to saw through the big rope.

18   By this time all seven tigers, the two lions, the rhinoceros, and the gorilla, along with countless screeching monkeys, were on their way across the crocodiles. There was still a lot of rope to cut through.

19   "Oh, hurry," the dragon kept saying.

20   Suddenly the animals' screaming grew louder and madder. When my father looked around, he saw that the first crocodile had finished his lollipop and started swimming down the river. The second crocodile hadn't finished yet, so he followed right after the first, still licking his lollipop. All the rest did the same, until they were all swimming away in a line. The seven tigers, the rhinoceros, the two lions, the gorilla, and the countless screeching monkeys were riding down the middle of the river on the train of crocodiles.

21   My father and the dragon laughed themselves weak. When my father finished cutting the rope, the baby dragon raced around in circles and tried to turn a somersault. But my father was in a hurry to fly away, and when the dragon finally calmed down a bit, my father climbed up onto his back.

22   "Where shall we go?" asked the dragon.

23   "We'll spend the night on the beach, and tomorrow we'll start on the long journey home," shouted my father. The dragon soared above the dark jungle and the muddy river and all the animals bellowing and all the crocodiles licking pink lollipops.

1   Part A

Who is narrating this story?

A   the dragon's father

B   one of the monkeys

C   an unknown third person

D   a child of the main character

Part B

Based on the answer to Part A, how does the narrator know what happened?

A   The narrator is simply the voice of the author.

B   The narrator's father told the story to him or her.

C   The narrator is the main character, now grown up.

D   The narrator was watching the action from a nearby tree.

2   Part A

What is the main character trying to do in this story?

A   rescue a baby dragon

B   fly home from an island

C   cross a river and walk home

D   make friends with crocodiles

Part B

What obstacle does the main character face to do this?

A   He has to cross the river.

B   He has to feed the crocodiles.

C   He has to talk to the gorilla.

D   He has to climb a rope.

3 Part A

What did the main character decide NOT to do?

A   take the baby dragon home

B   give lollipops to the crocodiles

C   call the baby dragon from across the river

D   use his jackknife to cut the rope on the dragon

Part B

Based on the answer to Part A, what might have happened if the main character had done that?

A   The gorilla would have heard him.

B   The crocodiles might have eaten him.

C   The tigers would have chased him.

D   The dragon would have run out of the bushes.

Guided Practice

Read the passage and answer the questions that follow.

Roebling's Bridge

by Jason Banks

See page 25
Focus Lesson:
Expository Text

1 John A. Roebling came to the United States from Germany in 1831. He was an engineer who helped settle the farming town of Saxonburg in western Pennsylvania. He soon began to work on a canal system that would allow water travel across the state. One problem with this system was the way the boats had to be pulled over steep hills. The hemp rope sometimes broke. To solve this problem, Roebling invented a strong, bendable wire rope. He received a patent for the cable in 1842, and started a company to make wire cable.

2 Roebling soon found more uses for his invention. He helped build the first wire-cable suspension bridge across the Allegheny River into Pittsburgh in 1845. A suspension bridge is one in which the roadway is hung on cables held up by towers. Roebling developed a way to spin the heavy wire cables at the building site and invented a simple and safe way to anchor them. This made it possible to build long suspension bridges. Roebling's Delaware Aqueduct, which opened in 1848, is the oldest surviving suspension bridge in America.

3 For a long time, New Yorkers had wanted a bridge to link Manhattan and Brooklyn. They were two of the country's largest cities in 1860. (Brooklyn and Manhattan did not join together to create modern New York City until 1898.) Many people thought it would be impossible to build such a long bridge. They thought it would fall down. However, in late 1866, a private project called The New York Bridge Company was started. John Roebling was hired as chief engineer to design the new bridge.

4 Roebling planned to make a suspension bridge with steel wire, which allowed it to be stronger, larger, and longer than any iron bridge yet built. The bridge would have a cable car, as well as roadways and a walkway. The project was approved and began in 1869.

5   However, soon after construction of the Brooklyn Bridge began, Roebling's foot was badly hurt in an accident on the bridge site. He developed a serious infection, and in those days doctors didn't have medicine to cure it. John Roebling died. Roebling's son and partner, Washington A. Roebling, was named chief engineer in his place.

6   There were several problems during the building of the bridge. An explosion and a fire slowed down construction. One of the companies sold them poor-quality wire. All the problems slowed down the project. But worst of all, Washington Roebling became seriously ill.

7   Washington Roebling had helped develop special containers used in building the foundations that would support the towers. The containers, called caissons, kept the workers dry when they worked under the water. Compressed air was pumped into the caissons. However, if the workers moved out of a caisson and its compressed air too quickly, they became ill. At the time, people didn't know what caused the illness. Washington Roebling was injured this way several times. He became so disabled that he had to stay in bed, and was unable to work at the bridge site anymore. The people who had thought it foolish to try to build the bridge in the first place now said, "I told you so!" But he did not give up on the project.

8   Roebling's wife, Emily, took up the work on the bridge. She had learned a great deal about engineering and construction. She carried messages and directions back and forth between the bedridden chief engineer and his staff. This went on for 11 years!

9   When finished, the stone towers stood 277 feet above water. Then work began on the cables to suspend the bridge's roadway. The workers used the longest and heaviest cables that had ever been made. They were made the same way John Roebling had made his cables. The job was so big that it took 18 months just to make the cables. When it came time to finally build the deck that would hold the roadways, a new kind of steel was available. This was a big improvement over iron because it made the bridge much stronger. Then more supports were added. Finally, John Roebling's son could look at the finished bridge his father had designed. Emily Roebling was the first person to cross the bridge.

10   When it was completed in 1883, the bridge was 1,595.5 feet long. It was by far the longest suspension bridge in the world. It still stands today as a reminder of the dreams, determination, and hard work of the Roebling family and all the workers who built it.

1 Part A

Why did some people think the Brooklyn Bridge couldn't be built?

_____

_____

_____

_____

> Reread paragraphs 3 and 4. What did people think about the idea of building the bridge?

Part B

What invention of John Roebling's helped overcome the problem from Part A?

_____

_____

_____

_____

> Read paragraph 1 again. What was different about the materials Roebling planned to use for the new bridge? How did he improve the materials for the new project?

2 Part A

What happened to Washington Roebling that could have kept him from finishing the Brooklyn Bridge?

_____

_____

_____

_____

> Read paragraphs 7 and 8 again. What happened during the building of the bridge?

Part B

Was the bridge ever finished?

_____

_____

_____

_____

> Reread paragraph 9. Did Roebling overcome his problem? If so, how did he solve it? Was there someone who could help him?

3   Part A

What can you tell about the bridge from the photograph?

_____

_____

_____

_____

Look closely at the photograph. What does the bridge look like? How is it different from other bridges?

Part B

Which paragraph explains about the type of bridge shown in the picture?

_____

_____

The paragraph does not have to be about the Brooklyn Bridge. It just has to tell about the type of bridge.

Commander Mark Polansky

by Chris Smith

1   Former astronaut Mark Polansky was born and raised in New Jersey. As a child, Polansky loved to follow the NASA missions that allowed humans to land on the moon. He decided he wanted to be like the astronauts, and his career path was set.

2   "When I was growing up, it was way back in the 1960s. It was the beginning of human spaceflight, and I got pretty excited," he said. "Back then, when I was in school and there would be a launch, they would stop classes, roll in a little black-and-white TV, and you'd get to watch everything live.

3   "And like any kid, you say, 'Hey, I want to be an astronaut when I grow up!' I sort of just never outgrew that."

4   Polansky worked hard in school. He began making his dream a reality when he was in college at Purdue University. An astronaut who had walked on the moon, Gene Cernan, had graduated from Purdue. Polansky met Cernan when the astronaut visited the school. Meeting a real astronaut made the idea seem like a realistic goal.

5   "I got to meet Gene Cernan during his visit to the dorm I lived in, and it got me thinking, 'You know, this is something that a guy could do,' " he said. But Polansky knew it wouldn't happen by itself. "I got thinking about the background of the astronauts and I started to pursue Air Force officer training for a career in the Air Force." He joined the Reserve Officer Training Corps (ROTC), so that when he graduated, he would have the training he needed to enter the Air Force as an officer.

6   In college, Polansky took special engineering courses for flying and space travel. After he graduated, he went on for a master's degree. Then he trained to become an Air Force test pilot. In 1992, he went to work for NASA as an aerospace engineer and research pilot. While he was not yet an astronaut, his main job was to teach astronauts to fly trainer jets and land the space shuttle.

7   The space shuttle was a reusable space craft used between 1981 and 2011. It took off from a vertical position, like a rocket, but it landed like a jet, on a runway. The shuttle orbited Earth and was used to launch satellites and conduct experiments. It allowed astronauts to build and service the International Space Station. It also launched the Hubble Space Telescope.

8   In 1996, NASA selected Polansky as an astronaut. In 2001, he flew his first mission as pilot on the Space Shuttle *Atlantis*. The flight of the *Atlantis* was an early visit to the International Space Station. The crew of that mission added the US laboratory *Destiny* to the station. The shuttle spent seven days docked to the station while *Destiny* was attached. Members of the crew made three spacewalks to complete the job. The crew also had to move a docking port. They delivered supplies and equipment to the crew staying on the space station.

9   In 2006, Polansky was made commander of the shuttle *Discovery* for a 12-day mission to the space station. The crew completed four spacewalks to make more improvements to the space station and to fix a solar panel that wouldn't fold up properly. Polansky and his crew also delivered a new crew member to the station and took needed supplies and equipment. They also brought home more than two tons of items that were no longer needed on the space station.

10   "I don't see us proceeding on when we haven't finished what we've started," Polansky said after the mission. "We need to go ahead and finish the International Space Station. And once that's all done, then hopefully we'll be in a position to look forward to a crew exploration vehicle, launching that successfully, going back to the moon, and moving on to bigger and better things with Mars. I just see this as a continuation, a process that gets us farther and farther along the road of exploration."

11   Polansky's third space shuttle mission was as commander on the *Endeavour*, in 2009. The shuttle crew delivered supplies, including special batteries, spare parts, and water. While the shuttle was docked at the space station, there were a record 13 astronauts working there. The astronauts were from all five International Space Station partners. In addition to NASA, there were astronauts from the Russian Space Agency, the Canadian Space Agency, the European Space Agency, and the Japanese Space Agency.

12   Asked whether it was difficult working in space, Polansky said, "It's much harder for people on the ground. Loved ones don't know when their people are coming home."

UNIT 2 Determination   93

13 In his last assignment at NASA, Polansky served as director of operations at the Gagarin Cosmonaut Training Center in Star City, Russia. He retired from NASA in 2012. In all, he had spent more than 40 days in space, doing what he loved.

1   Part A

What first inspired Polansky to become an astronaut?

A   meeting astronaut Gene Cernan at college

B   following the NASA missions on television as a boy

C   studying the early space shuttle launches in college

D   watching movies about space exploration in high school

Part B

Which sentence supports that first inspiration of Polansky's career?

A   "Meeting a real astronaut made the idea seem like a realistic goal."

B   "After he graduated, he went on for a master's degree."

C   "He decided he wanted to be like the astronauts, and his career path was set."

D   "In college, Polansky took special engineering courses for flying and space travel."

2   Part A

How did meeting astronaut Gene Cernan help Polansky's career?

A   It made him see the idea as a realistic goal.

B   It made him see how much work he had to do.

C   Cernan recommended him for pilot training.

D   Cernan made him switch to engineering classes.

Part B

Based on the answer to Part A, what was the next step Polansky took toward preparing for his career?

A getting a job with NASA

B joining Air Force ROTC

C becoming a research pilot

D studying for his master's degree

3 Part A

What is the main idea of the article?

A Not just anyone can grow up to be a space shuttle astronaut.

B When you see something interesting, you can make it your career.

C Space missions are much harder on the families than on the astronauts.

D When you know what career you want, you can find ways to make it work.

Part B

Which details about Polansky's choices support the main idea?

A He went from pilot to commander and, by the end of his career, he had spent more than 40 days in space.

B He worked hard in school, talked with an astronaut, and found out about the background of the astronauts.

C Cernan had graduated from Purdue University and later became an astronaut who walked on the moon.

D He flew his first mission on the Space Shuttle *Atlantis,* and later worked on the International Space Station.

Guided Practice

Read the passage and answer the questions that follow.

The Kids' State Dinner Speeches

See page 25
Focus Lesson:
Expository Text

First Lady Michelle Obama held a formal state dinner at the White House for winners of a nationwide healthy foods recipe contest for children. She and President Barack Obama spoke to the children before the dinner.

First Lady Michelle Obama:

1   I want to thank and recognize the stars of today's show—the 54 winners of the Healthy Lunchtime Challenge! Our stars. We have seen that when kids get involved in creating healthy meals, the results can be amazing and delicious and fun. You'll come up with ideas that none of us grownups ever thought of. You'll find new ways to get your families and friends to eat healthy and try new foods.

2   I know that all of you have been motivated by different events in your life, different people in your life, to cook healthy and to make changes. And some of you might even start your own online cooking show. Maybe you'll start making appearances on local TV newscasts. I know some of you have already started doing that—like our winner from Washington State. Amber, where are you? You've been making the TV rounds? Pretty spectacular!

3   We know that if you're able to eat healthy foods, if you have more opportunities to get up and be active, that's all part of it. We all know that— got to get up and move. And if you're surrounded by parents and teachers and community leaders who encourage you to live healthier lives, then there's no telling what you'll achieve.

4   That's why we're working with schools and health professionals to teach you about making good choices—not just at home, but in school as well. Because we know sometimes you get to school, you lose your mind, right? We're working on that. It's why we're working with restaurants and food companies and grocery stores, so that you have healthy options that give you the energy you need to succeed in school and in life.

5   Because in the end, it isn't just about what happens in the kitchen or at the dinner table. It's about making sure your body can be strong and healthy, and your mind can be ready to learn and explore and dream, today and for years to come. This is about giving you the foundation to fly high and dream big.

President Barack Obama:

6   Well, hello, everybody!

7   Now, first of all, usually at a state dinner, I get invited. So I don't know what happened on this one—somehow the invitation slipped through somewhere.

8   I wanted to come by, first of all, because everybody looks very nice—you guys all got dressed up. Second of all, I hear the food is pretty good.

9   You're setting a great example for your classmates, and I suspect you're setting a good example for your parents, who sometimes may not be eating as healthy as they're supposed to. So you're really making a difference in all the communities and all the states all across the country. We could not be prouder of you.

10   Frankly, I'm not a great cook—I'm not bad, but I don't do it that much. It's hard to find the time. But when I do cook, I'm following a recipe. And to think that all of you have invented all this fabulous food just shows how creative you are and it shows that food that tastes good can be healthy, too. Because I think sometimes we get thinking that if it's good for you then it must be nasty. But when things that are good for you don't taste very good, it's usually because they're not prepared right.

11   So I will just tell you a story. When I was a kid, my family, when they cooked vegetables, they just boiled them. And the vegetables got all soft and mushy, and nobody wanted to eat peas or Brussels sprouts because they were mush. And broccoli, too. And now I actually like vegetables because they're prepared right. And so you guys are getting a jump on things because you're figuring that out earlier.

12   So I just want to say to all of the young people here, keep it up. You guys are going to set a good example for everybody, all across the country. You're eating healthy, and you're out there being active and playing sports and you're out on the playground. Not only are you going to have a better life, but you're also helping to create a stronger, healthier America.

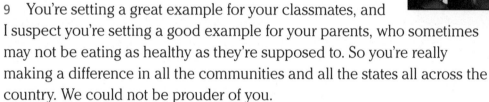

Here's one of the winning recipes in the Healthy Lunchtime Challenge you can try.

Tortilla Bowl Deluxe

Ingredients

- 4 ounce boneless chicken breast, cut into bite-size pieces
- $\frac{1}{4}$ cup diced avocado
- $\frac{1}{4}$ cup diced orange bell pepper
- $\frac{1}{4}$ cup diced tomato
- $\frac{1}{4}$ cup shredded Monterey Jack cheese
- Salt and freshly ground black pepper
- 1 corn tortilla bowl

Preparation

1 In a medium bowl, toss together the pieces of chicken, avocado, bell pepper, tomato, and cheese.

2 Add salt and pepper.

3 Scoop mixture into the tortilla bowl, and serve immediately.

1 Part A

What is different about the two speeches?

_____

_____

_____

_____

> Reread the speeches. What does the First Lady talk about in her speech? What does the President say that is different?

Part B

What is an example of something that President Obama said that is different from what the First Lady said?

_____

_____

_____

> Reread paragraphs 10 and 11 of his speech carefully. How is this different from what the First Lady talked about?

2   Part A

What was the purpose of the Healthy Lunchtime Challenge?

_____

_____

_____

_____

> Reread the first two paragraphs of First Lady Michelle Obama's speech. What was the Healthy Lunchtime Challenge?

Part B

In Michelle Obama's speech, what reasons did she give for holding the contest?

_____

_____

_____

_____

> Review paragraph 1. Why did First Lady Michelle Obama hold the contest?

3 Part A

What steps are involved in the recipe for Tortilla Bowl Deluxe?

_____

_____

_____

_____

> Read the recipe and look for directions. How do you make this dish?

Part B

Based on your answer to Part A, what does the word *dice* mean in the recipe?

_____

_____

_____

_____

> Review the preparation instructions to figure out what the words mean. The word *dice* can have multiple meanings.

Wild Animals of Alaska

by John Maverick

1   It's not easy for animals to survive in Alaska's cold, snowy climate. Animals that live there have adapted to the cold by growing special fur, feathers, or fat. Some have learned to put away food for the winter while others go into hibernation, sleeping through the coldest months. Even so, each animal must brave the cold weather and work hard to find food and shelter for itself and its young. Here are just a few of the animals that live in Alaska.

2   **Wood Frog** The wood frog is one of the few amphibians found in Alaska. Wood frogs live in grasslands, forests, and even tundras. They're dark (to absorb heat from the sun), and about three inches long. They hibernate in old vegetation during the cold winters. They eat insects and small animals.

3   **Wolf** Wolves live in a variety of habitats covering 85 percent of Alaska. They range in color from black to almost white. They are highly social animals that live in packs with an alpha male and an alpha female. Wolves build dens in the sides of hills and have four to seven pups. The range of a pack can be 200 to 600 square miles. Wolves hunt moose, deer, mountain goats, beavers, hares, and other animals, including fish and birds. Wolves help keep down the population of the animals they hunt.

4   **Red Fox** The red fox is found throughout Alaska. It is related to the wolf since both are members of the dog family. Red foxes always have a white tip on their tail, but can range in color from red to silver to black. Like wolves, foxes build dens in which to have their kits. They eat rodents, hares, squirrels, birds, eggs, insects, plants, and meat. They store some of their food for later use. They can become quite tame if they have contact with people.

5   **Sea Otter** The sea otter is a relative to the mink and the land otter, and lives throughout the coastal waters of Alaska. Its hind feet are webbed and its fur is very dense, or thick. The otter relies on trapped air in its fur to keep it warm in the cold water. Sea otters are good swimmers and divers, and can hold their

breath for four minutes. They eat clams, crab, fish, and octopus. They have one pup in late spring, which may hitch a ride on its mother's chest. Otters are skillful with their front paws, cracking clams with rocks.

6   **Gray Whale** Gray whales migrate between California and Alaska every year. That's a 10,000-mile journey! Newborn calves are 16 feet long and weigh 1,500 pounds. Gray whales are bottom feeders, lying on their sides and filtering tiny crustaceans through the baleen plates in their mouths. In the 1800s and 1900s, gray whales were hunted almost to extinction. The International Convention for the Regulation of Whaling in 1946 protected the whales, so that their population has greatly increased.

7   **Polar Bear** The polar bear is a marine mammal that lives most of its life in the water. Polar bears live near the ice pack, migrating with it in the spring and fall. They have hollow hair to aid swimming, a white coat, and hairy feet. Female polar bears build a den in drifting snow and give birth to two cubs in December. They don't come out of the den until late March or April. Polar bears eat seals, walruses, and beluga whales. They are also scavengers that eat dead meat.

8   **Moose** The moose is the largest member of the deer family. Moose thrive in forests and river thickets. Only bulls have antlers, which they use in courtship displays. Young are born as twins, and leave their mother after a year. Moose only migrate up to 60 miles. They eat willow, birch, aspen, pond weeds, and grasses. Their main defense is running, which can be difficult in deep snow. The deep snow can make it difficult for them to find food. Because of this, moose sometimes live in urban areas and may eat fruit trees and gardens.

9   **Muskox** Muskox are related to sheep and goats. They have changed little since the Ice Age and are well adapted to living on the Arctic tundra, a frozen, treeless plain. Muskox have long hair with fine underfur. Both male and female muskox have horns. They are very social animals, living in herds with a dominant male. They protect their young by forming a line or circle with their horned heads outward, toward the threat. Muskox eat a variety of grasses and woody plants. To eat, they must seek out areas where the snow has blown away in the winter.

1   **Part A**

Which Alaskan animal hibernates in the winter?

A   polar bear

B   wood frog

C   sea otter

D   red fox

Part B

In what other way has the animal in Part A adapted to the Alaskan climate?

A   It has dark skin to absorb the heat.

B   It burrows into the snow for warmth.

C   It migrates to California for the winter.

D   It is white so it blends in with the snow.

2 **Part A**

Which animal is a relative of the wolf?

A   red fox

B   muskox

C   moose

D   sea otter

Part B

According to the passage, what does this animal have in common with the wolf?

A   It builds a den.

B   It eats rodents.

C   It lives in a pack.

D   It can become tame.

3 Part A

What is the main idea of the article?

A   Alaska has a rich mixture of wildlife.

B   The land in Alaska is harsh and wild.

C   Many Alaskan animals have difficult lives.

D   Many Alaskan animals are near extinction.

Part B

What key detail best supports the answer to Part A?

A   Otters are skillful with their front paws.

B   Polar bears must migrate each spring and fall.

C   Deep snow can make it difficult for moose to find food.

D   Muskox are well adapted to living in such a cold place.

Unit 3 Discoveries

 ## Lesson 1

Literary Text focuses on an explorer's discoveries around the world and a little girl's discoveries in her own neighborhood.

 ## Lesson 2

Literary Text shares the discoveries of a poet who pays attention to the world around him. You also meet a boy that discovers that he already has what he was looking for.

 ## Lesson 3

Informational Text focuses on seeing important places through the lens of a camera. You also learn about the discoveries in the world of science.

 ## Lesson 4

Informational Text focuses on the worlds under the sea and in the heavens above.

Guided Practice

Read the passage and answer the questions that follow.

Discovering Vinland

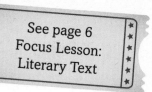

See page 6
Focus Lesson:
Literary Text

1   Eric the Red had lived in Greenland for 20 years. His son Leif had grown into a tall, sturdy man. One spring Leif said to his father, "I have never seen Norway, our motherland. I long to go there and meet the great men and see the places about which you have told me." And so Leif went.

2   But as he sailed again to go back home, his voyage was unexpectedly interrupted. Leif had had good luck until he was past Iceland. Then great winds came out of the north and tossed his ship about like a plaything. The ship was blown south for days and days, until the men did not know where they were. Finally, they saw land.

3   Leif steered for it immediately, and when they landed the men threw themselves upon the ground. "I never lay on a bed as soft as this grass," one said. "Taller trees do not grow in Norway," said another.

4   "I never saw so fertile a land," Leif said. "There is no stone here as in Norway, but only good black dirt."

5   They stayed many days in this country and explored what was there. A man named Tyrker was on the voyage. He had taken care of Leif when he was a little boy, so Leif loved him. One evening, when the men came back to camp, Leif looked around on his comrades, he said, "Where is Tyrker?"

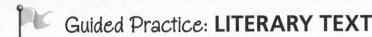

6   No one knew, and that made Leif angry. "Is a man of so little value in this empty land that you would lose one?" he said. Then he turned and started out to hunt for him, and his men followed, feeling silent and ashamed. They had not gone far when they saw Tyrker running toward them, laughing and talking to himself.

7   Leif put his arms about him and said, "Where have you been?"

8   "I have not been so very far, but I have found something wonderful," Tyrker said. "I have found grapes growing wild!"

9   "It cannot be," Leif said in astonishment. Grapes do not grow in Greenland, nor in Iceland, nor even in Norway, so it seemed a delightful thing to the Norsemen.

10   "Can I not tell grapes when I see them?" cried Tyrker. "Did I not grow up in Germany, where every hillside is covered with grapevines? Ah, it seems like my old home."

11   "It is beyond belief," Leif said. "I have heard travelers tell of seeing grapes growing, but I myself have never seen it. You shall take us to them early in the morning, Tyrker."

12   So in the morning they went back into the woods and found the grapes. They ate of them, and they were well pleased.

13   Later that afternoon Leif told the men, "Winter will soon be coming on, and the sea about Greenland will be freezing up. We must begin our journey home. I mean to take some of the bounty of this land to show to our people. We will fill the rowboat with grapes and tow it behind us, and the ship we will load with logs from these great trees."

14   As they sailed away, Leif looked back at the verdant shore and said, "I will call this country Vinland for the grapes that grow there."

15   For all that voyage they had fair weather and sailed into Eric the Red's harbor well before the winter came. Eric saw the ship and ran down to the shore. He took Leif into his arms and said, "Oh, my son, my old eyes ached to see you, and I hunger to hear of all that you have seen and done."

16   "Luck has followed me all the way," said Leif. "See what I have brought home."

17   "Lumber!" cried his father. "It is better stuff than gold!"

18   Then Eric's men saw the grapes and tasted them. "Surely you must have plundered Asgard," they said, smacking their lips.

19 At the feast that night, Leif told them all about their adventure in Vinland. "No man would ever need a cloak there, and the soil is richer than the soil of Norway. Grain grows wild, and you yourselves saw the grapes that we got from there. The forests are without end and the sea is full of fish."

20 Years later, a wise man wrote down the story of those voyages and of Vinland, and people read the tales and enjoyed them. But no one remembered where the place was. It all seemed like a fairy tale; but long afterwards, scholars began to read those stories with wide-open eyes and to wonder. They talked and argued together and studied various lands and coastlines and read the stories over and over.

21 At last the sages have come to believe that Vinland was on the eastern shore of North America. And the people have put up statues of Leif Ericsson, the Norseman who came to America 1,000 years ago.

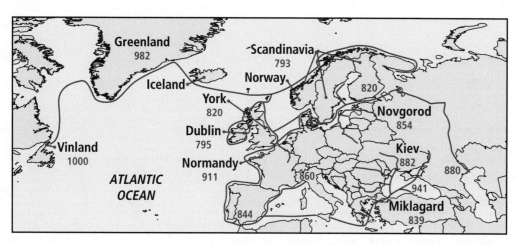

Voyages of the Vikings from 793–1000 A.D.

1   Part A

What is the theme of this story?

_____

_____

_____

> A theme can be a lesson that the author is trying to teach readers. What lesson do you think Leif Erickson learned from his experience?

Part B

What sentence supports your answer to Part A?

_____

_____

_____

_____

> Reread paragraph 4. How does Leif Erickson feel about Vinland? How does it compare to his homeland?

2   Part A

Where was Leif Erickson traveling to when he landed on Vinland?

_____

_____

_____

> Reread the beginning of the story. Where did Leif Erickson live, and where did he want to go?

Part B

Why did the author include the map with this story?

_____

_____

_____

> Find Greenland and Norway on the map. Where is Vinland? What can you learn from this map?

3   Part A

What can you tell about Leif Erickson from the story?

_____

_____

_____

_____

_____

_____

> Reread the story. Notice what Leif Erickson says and does. What can you tell about his character? How does he treat people?

Part B

Which sentence supports your answer to Part A?

_____

_____

_____

> Read paragraphs 5–8. What does Leif do in the story that reveals something about his character?

A Mysterious Neighbor

Adapted from *The Girl Next Door*
by Augusta Huiell Seaman

1   The two girls put on their hats and strolled out for their usual afternoon walk and treat of ice-cream soda. But they had gone no farther from their own door than the length of the Benedict brick wall when they were suddenly brought to a halt in front of the closed gate by hearing a sound on the other side of it. It was a sound of someone's struggle to open it—the click of a key turning and turning in the lock and the rattling of the iron knob. Janet and Marcia heard then the sound of a voice murmuring: "Oh, dear! What *shall* I do? I can't get this open!"

2   As the friends watched, out stepped a girl. The face was the one that had appeared in the upper window. On her arm she carried a small market-basket, and her eyes had a confused, almost frightened, look.

3   Marcia and Janet stood waiting to see which way their neighbor would turn. But the girl only stood, her back to the gate, looking uncertainly to the right and left. She noticed them and suddenly seemed to make a decision.

4   "Oh, please, *could* you tell me how to find this?" she asked, holding out a slip of paper. Marcia hurried to her side and read the written address. And when she had read it, she realized that it was the little grocery-shop on the other side of town where she had once encountered Miss Benedict.

5   "Why, certainly!" she cried. "You walk over five blocks in that direction, then turn to your left and down three. You can't miss it; it's right next to a shoemaker's place."

6   The girl looked more confused than ever. Her eyes turned to the busy street-crossing near which they stood, crowded with hurrying trucks and automobiles.

7   "Thank you!" she faltered. "Do I go this way?" And then, with sudden candor, "You see, I'm strange in these streets." Her voice was clear and pretty, but her accent markedly un-American. Both girls half consciously noted it.

8   "Well," said Marcia; "would you like us to take you there? We're not going in any special direction, and I've been there before."

9   The girl looked relieved. "Oh, *would* you be so kind? I'm just—just scared to death on these streets!"

10   They turned to walk with her, one on each side, and got her safely across the busy avenue. Then, in the quiet stretch of the next block, they walked together in complete and embarrassing silence. It was a silence that Marcia and Janet had fully expected their companion to break—possibly to reveal some reason for her errand and her strangeness in the streets. They didn't want to ask her questions that might seem rude. But the girl said nothing. The strain at last became too much for Janet.

11   "I don't blame you for feeling nervous in these city streets," she began. "I'm a country girl myself, and I act like a scared rabbit whenever I go out alone here."

12   The girl turned to Janet. "I've never been out in them alone before," she said. Then there was another silence during which Marcia and Janet both searched in their minds for something else to say. But it was the girl herself who broke the silence the second time.

13   "Thank you for your music the other day," she said, turning to Marcia. "I heard you. I often hear you and listen."

14   "Oh, I'm so glad you liked it!" cried Marcia. "Do you care for music?"

15   "I adore it," she replied simply.

16   "Look here!" exclaimed Marcia, suddenly; "how did you know I was playing the violin?"

17   "Because I've watched you often—through the shutters!"

18   Marcia and Janet exchanged glances. So the watching was not all on *their* side of the fence! This was surprising news!

19   "That last thing you played the other day—will you—will you tell me what it was?" went on their new companion, shyly.

20   "Why, that was Schumann's 'Träumerei,'" answered Marcia. "I love it, don't you?"

21   "Yes but I never heard it before; that is, I never *remember* hearing it, and yet—somehow I seemed to *know* it. I can't think why. I don't understand. It's as if I'd *dreamed* it, I think."

22   Marcia and Janet again exchanged glances. What a strange child this was, who talked of having "dreamed" music that was quite familiar to almost every one.

23 "Perhaps you heard it at a concert," suggested Janet.

24 "I never went to a concert," she replied, much to their amazement. And then, noticing their surprise, she added: "You see, I've always lived 'way off in the country, in just a little village—till now."

25 "Oh—yes," answered Janet, pretending she understood, though in truth she and Marcia were more confused than ever.

26 But by this time they had reached the little grocery-shop, and all three went inside while their new friend made her purchases. These she read off slowly from a slip of paper, and the grocer packed them in her basket. But when it came to paying for them and making change, she was again confused and nervous.

27 "I think you said these eggs were a shilling?" she said to the grocer.

28 "Shilling—no! I said they were a quarter," he said impatiently.

29 "A quarter?" she asked, and turned questioning eyes to her two friends.

30 "He means this," said Marcia, picking out a 25-cent piece from the change the girl held.

31 "Oh, thank you! I don't understand this American money," she explained. And Marcia and Janet added another question to their rapidly growing mental list.

32 On the way back home, however, she grew silent again, and though the girls chatted back and forth about quite impersonal subjects—the crowded streets, the warm weather, the sights they passed,—she was not talkative. And the nearer they drew to their homes, the more depressed she appeared to become.

1 Part A

Which word best describes the girl Janet and Marcia meet?

A curious

B foolish

C pleasant

D unusual

Part B

Which sentence from the story best supports your answer to Part A?

A "'Oh, please, *could* you tell me how to find this?' she asked, holding out a slip of paper."

B "These she read off slowly from a slip of paper, and the grocer packed them in her basket."

C "What a strange child this was, who talked of having 'dreamed' music that was quite familiar to almost every one."

D "And when she had read it, she realized that it was the little grocery-shop on the other side of town where she had once encountered Miss Benedict."

2 Part A

What do Janet and the girl have in common?

A They are from the country.

B They like to listen to music.

C They speak a different language.

D They enjoy making conversation.

Part B

In which paragraph did you find the answer to Part A?

A paragraph 7

B paragraph 10

C paragraph 11

D paragraph 15

3 Part A

Which is the best summary of this story?

A A neighbor tells Janet that she likes to listen to her music, and she sometimes looks through the shutters to watch Janet play the violin.

B A neighbor seems happy when Janet and Marcia take her to the grocery store, but she becomes more quiet and sad as they approach her home.

C Janet and Marcia meet their neighbor and walk her to the grocery store because she does not know where it is. The girl is different from anyone they have ever met.

D Janet and Marcia meet their neighbor, who is unfamiliar with the city. They take her to the grocery store and help her figure out how much money she needs to pay for her groceries.

Part B

Which sentence from the story best supports your answer to Part A?

A "So the watching was not all on *their* side of the fence!"

B "Marcia and Janet stood waiting to see which way their neighbor would turn."

C "Then, in the quiet stretch of the next block, they walked together in complete and embarrassing silence."

D "The two girls put on their hats and strolled out for their usual afternoon walk and treat of ice-cream soda."

Guided Practice

Read the poem and answer the questions that follow.

The Wonderful World
by William Brighty Rands

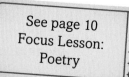
See page 10
Focus Lesson:
Poetry

1 Great, wide, beautiful, wonderful World,
With the wonderful water round you curled,
And the wonderful grass upon your breast,
World, you are beautifully drest.

2 The wonderful air is over me.
And the wonderful wind is shaking the tree—
It walks on the water, and whirls the mills,
And talks to itself on the top of the hills.

3 You friendly Earth, how far do you go,
With the wheat-fields that nod and the rivers that flow,
With cities and gardens, and cliffs and isles,
And people upon you for thousands of miles?

4 Ah! you are so great, and I am so small,
I hardly can think of you, World, at all;
And yet, when I said my prayers today,
A whisper within me seemed to say:
"You are more than the Earth, though you are such a dot!
You can love and think, and the Earth can not."

1   Part A

What two words does the speaker use often?

_____

_____

> Reread the poem and its title. Look for words that are used more than once.

Part B

What effect does the repetition of these words have on the reader?

_____

_____

> Keep in mind that the speaker uses these words to describe things on Earth. Why do you think these words are repeated?

2   Part A

Why does the speaker conclude that he is more than the Earth?

_____

_____

_____

> Reread the end of the poem. The speaker of the poem says that he hears a whisper within him that tells him why he is more than the Earth. How is he different than Earth?

Part B

Which line of the poem states or supports your answer to Part A?

_____

_____

_____

> Read the last stanza again. Is there any line that supports your answer?

3   Part A

How would this poem be different if it were written as a drama?

_____

_____

_____

> Remember that a drama is a play. What would this poem have that it does not have now?

Part B

How would this poem be different if it were written as a short story?

_____

_____

_____

> A poem has a speaker. What does a short story have?

Read the passage and answer the questions that follow.

The Golden Windows

by Laura E. Richards

1   All day long the little boy worked hard, in field and barn and shed, for his people were poor farmers, and could not pay a workman; but at sunset there came an hour that was all his own, for his father had given it to him. Then the boy would go up to the top of a hill and look across at another hill that rose some miles away.

2   On this far hill stood a house with windows of clear gold and diamonds. They shone and blazed so that it made the boy wink to look at them: but after a while the people in the house put up shutters, as it seemed, and then it looked like any common farmhouse. The boy supposed they did this because it was supper-time; and then he would go into the house and have his supper of bread and milk, and go to bed.

3   One day the boy's father called him and said: "You have been a good boy, and have earned a holiday. Take this day for your own; try to learn some good thing."

4   The boy thanked his father and kissed his mother; then he put a piece of bread in his pocket, and started off to find the house with the golden windows.

5   It was pleasant walking. His bare feet made marks in the white dust, and when he looked back, the footprints seemed to be following him, and making company for him. His shadow, too, kept beside him, and would dance or run with him as he pleased; so it was very cheerful.

6   By and by he felt hungry; and he sat down by a brown brook that ran through the alder hedge by the roadside, and ate his bread, and drank the clear water. Then he scattered the crumbs for the birds, as his mother had taught him to do, and went on his way.

7   After a long time he came to a high green hill; and when he had climbed the hill, there was the house on the top; but it seemed that the shutters were up, for he could not see the golden windows. He came up to the house, and then he could well have wept, for the windows were of clear glass, like any others, and there was no gold anywhere about them.

8   A woman came to the door, and looked kindly at the boy, and asked him what he wanted.

9   "I saw the golden windows from our hilltop," he said, "and I came to see them, but now they are only glass."

10   The woman shook her head and laughed.

11   "We are poor farming people," she said, "and are not likely to have gold about our windows; but glass is better to see through."

12   She bade the boy sit down on the broad stone step at the door, and brought him a cup of milk and a cake, and bade him rest; then she called her daughter, a child of his own age, and nodded kindly at the two, and went back to her work.

13   The little girl was barefooted like himself, and wore a brown cotton gown, but her hair was golden like the windows he had seen, and her eyes were blue like the sky at noon. She led the boy about the farm, and showed him her black calf with the white star on its forehead, and he told her about his own at home, which was red like a chestnut, with four white feet. Then when they had eaten an apple together, and so had become friends, the boy asked her about the golden windows.

14   The little girl nodded, and said she knew all about them, only he had mistaken the house.

15   "You have come quite the wrong way!" she said. "Come with me, and I will show you the house with the golden windows, and then you will see for yourself."

16   They went to a knoll that rose behind the farmhouse, and as they went the little girl told him that the golden windows could only be seen at a certain hour, about sunset.

17   "Yes, I know that!" said the boy.

18   When they reached the top of the knoll, the girl turned and pointed; and there on a hill far away stood a house with windows of clear gold and diamond, just as he had seen them. And when they looked again, the boy saw that it was his own home.

19   Then he told the little girl that he must go. He gave her his best pebble, the white one with the red band. He had carried this pebble for a year in his pocket; and she gave him three horse-chestnuts, one red like satin, one spotted, and one white like milk. He kissed her, and promised to come again, but he did not tell her what he had learned; and so he went back down the hill, and the little girl stood in the sunset light and watched him.

20 The way home was long, and it was dark before the boy reached his father's house; but the lamplight and firelight shone through the windows, making them almost as bright as he had seen them from the hilltop; and when he opened the door, his mother came to kiss him, and his little sister ran to throw her arms about his neck, and his father looked up and smiled from his seat by the fire.

21 "Have you had a good day?" asked his mother.

22 Yes, the boy had had a very good day.

23 "And have you learned anything?" asked his father.

24 "Yes!" said the boy. "I have learned that our house has windows of gold and diamond."

1 Part A

What is the theme of this story?

A Be happy with what you have.

B It is good to learn a lesson on a holiday.

C It is nice to have some time for yourself.

D Treat others as you would like to be treated.

Part B

Which sentence from the story best supports your answer to Part A?

A "'You have been a good boy, and have earned a holiday.'"

B "He gave her his best pebble, the white one with the red band."

C "'I have learned that our house has windows of gold and diamond.'"

D "'Come with me, and I will show you the house with the golden windows, and then you will see for yourself.'"

2 Part A

What kept the boy company along his journey to find the house with the golden windows?

A the birds

B the sunset

C his thoughts

D his footprints

Part B

In which paragraph did you find your answer to Part A?

A paragraph 4

B paragraph 5

C paragraph 6

D paragraph 7

3 Part A

How are the boy and the girl in the story alike?

A They are very poor.

B They have gold hair.

C They work very hard.

D They have blue eyes.

Part B

Which line from the story supports your answer to Part A?

A "…her hair was golden like the windows he had seen…"

B "…and brought him a cup of milk and a cake, and bade him rest;"

C "The little girl was barefooted like himself, and wore a brown cotton gown…"

D "The little girl nodded, and said she knew all about them, only he had mistaken the house."

Guided Practice

Read the passage and answer the questions that follow.

The National Historic Landmark Photo Contest

See page 22
Focus Lesson:
Instructional Text

It's time to visit National Historic Landmarks and explore the stories that make our nation great.

- **Discover sports**—a baseball stadium, a racetrack, college bowls, and more.

- **Explore the sciences**—radar testing, a giant antenna, and a jet propulsion laboratory.

- **Appreciate the craftsmanship**—design schools, Gilded Age mansions, handcrafted cabins.

- **Understand the sacrifice**—battlefields, battleships, civil rights sites.

- **Feel the artistry**—studios, theaters, museums, and more.

- **Surprise the kid inside**—roller coasters, merry-go-rounds, and many trains.

- **Be inspired**—designed landscapes, religious buildings, and great vistas.

Fallingwater

National Historic Landmarks tell tales in neighborhoods, cities, parks, and landscapes all across the country. Get out your camera. Visit a site. Listen to the stories. Share your observations.

Rules and Entry Information

We invite you to share—in your own photographs and words—your experience of your favorite National Historic Landmarks (NHLs) across the country. This year's contest is open for entries from Monday, April 1, through Tuesday, July 9 (midnight EST).

Contest Purpose: The NHL Photo Contest is a free photography contest held each year by the National Historic Landmarks Program of the National Park Service (NPS) to raise awareness of and appreciation for our NHLs and the conscientious efforts of their owners and managers to preserve these places and objects for future generations. The Secretary of the Interior has designated more than 2,500 NHLs. A NHL is a place that tells an important story that relates to our nation's history.

Guidelines for Photography at National Historic Landmarks

After being sure the place is a National Historic Landmark, find out if the place is open to the public. Please do not trespass on private property. In the photo description space, please include the NHL name, city, state, and include an observation—either about the NHL itself, or about why you entered that photograph. You will need to read and agree to the contest rules before you can advance to the group page. Upload your image to the website.

USS *Constitution*

RULES:

1) All entries must be entered before the close of the contest on July 9.

2) All photographs that you enter must be your own work and you must own the rights to share the entry.

3) All eligible entries must show a National Historic Landmark. A list of NHLs can be found on the National Park Service website at www.nps.gov.

4) Only one image per NHL.

5) All entries must include the name and location of the NHL, the name of the photographer, and an email where the photographer can be reached.

6) Any entry including an individual in the photograph of the NHL must be accompanied by a photo release. However, this is required only if you can recognize the individual in the photograph. If the person is too far away for his or her face to be seen, a photo release is not needed. If your photo is selected, you will be required to provide a signed release form for any recognizable individual in your photograph.

7) Many NHLS are privately owned or located on private property. If the NHL is not open to the public, you must obtain and submit written permission from the property owner. Please do not enter onto NHL sites that are not open to the public without permission of the property owner.

8) By adding your entry to the 2013 NHL Photo contest, you authorize the National Park Service to:

- Use your entry for any educational and informational purposes forever.

- Crop or change your photograph or edit your text.

- Use your name and state where you live.

9) NPS is not responsible for lost, late, misdirected, or incomplete entries.

10) Judging is based on image quality and expressing the experience of visiting the NHL.

Contest Entries: If your photograph is chosen, you will be contacted by NPS staff in August. You must respond by email within seven days or another winner will be selected. Winners will be announced on the NPS.gov NHL Photo Contest page in September. All decisions are final.

1   **Part A**

What should a photographer do to determine if a place is a National Historic Landmark?

_____

_____

_____

> Look at the rules again. Which rule answers this question?

Part B

What should a photographer do right after he or she has determined that a place is a National Historic Landmark?

_____

_____

_____

> Read the article again carefully. What should the photographer do once he or she finds a National Historic Landmark to photograph?

2 Part A

What should the photographer do if he or she takes a picture of a person along with a National Historic Landmark?

_____

_____

> Carefully read Rule 6. What do you need to ask a person if you take a photograph of them?

Part B

When is the action taken in Part A not necessary?

_____

_____

_____

_____

> Try to remember the information given in Rule 6. If you can't remember, reread this rule.

3 Part A

What are two types of places that might be National Historic Landmarks?

_____

_____

_____

> Reread the beginning of the article. Many examples are given here.

Part B

Why would these places be National Historic Landmarks?

_____

_____

_____

_____

_____

> What is a National Historic Landmark? How does a place become recognized as one?

Read the passage and answer the questions that follow.

How Pollen Tells Us About Climate

by Ross Allen

1   People with allergies know what to expect when the flowers are blooming and the bees are buzzing. Every year around springtime, pollen spores cause problems for thousands of people. They suffer from runny noses, uncontrollable sneezing, and itchy, watery eyes. But how can these problematic spores help scientists learn about the climate in the past?

2   Pollen grains are the reproductive bodies of seed plants, including flowering plants. Each of these grains has its own special shape depending on what plant it comes from. The walls of the spores are very firm and strong.

3   When pollen grains are washed or blown into water, such as lakes or rivers, their tough outer walls protect them. The grains may sink into the mud at the bottoms of ponds, lakes, or oceans. They may stay in these layers of mud for thousands of years, the same way shells and plants sometimes do. Scientists can then sink a tube into the mud and lift out a core sample. This is like when you stick a straw into a milkshake, cover the top with your finger, and lift the straw. Some of the milkshake stays inside the straw. The scientists study the shapes of the pollen grains in the samples. They may find out what kinds of plants were growing at the time the grains sank to the bottom of the water. Knowing this helps the scientists to make educated guesses about the climate at that time. They use information about where plants grow now and in the past and the climates of those areas to understand more about the past.

4   Once they take a core sample, the scientists separate the pollen and spores from the rocks and other materials. They use both chemicals and special tools for this work. The grains are very small. Many thousands could fit on the head of a pin. The scientists count and label the grains using a microscope. They may create pictures and charts of the type and amount of pollen in their samples.

5   By studying pollen from dated core samples, scientists can create records of changes in plants going back for millions of years. Not only can pollen records tell us about the past climate, but they can also tell us how we are affecting our climate. Comparing changes in plants from the last few thousand years to recent changes can also help scientists understand how human actions have affected an environment.

1   Part A

Which statement about pollen grains is true?

A   They are very small.

B   They have soft walls.

C   They do not last long.

D   They do not sink in water.

Part B

Which sentence from the article supports your answer to Part A?

A   "Many thousands could fit on the head of a pin."

B   "Pollen grains are the reproductive bodies of seed plants including flowering plants."

C   "Each of these grains has its very own special shape depending on what plant it comes from."

D   "They may stay in these layers of mud for thousands of years the way shells and plants sometimes do."

2   Part A

Which organizational pattern best describes paragraph 3?

A   sequential

B   comparison

C   cause/effect

D   problem/solution

Part B

Which paragraph has the same organizational pattern as paragraph 3?

A   paragraph 1

B   paragraph 2

C   paragraph 4

D   paragraph 5

3   **Part A**

Read this sentence from the article.

> "But how can these problematic spores help scientists learn about the climate in the past?"

What does the word *problematic* mean?

A   spreads quickly

B   causes trouble

C   hard to find

D   lasts long

Part B

Which sentence helped you determine the meaning of *problematic*?

A   "They suffer from runny noses, uncontrollable sneezing, and itchy, watery eyes."

B   "Pollen grains are the reproductive bodies of seed plants including flowering plants."

C   "Each of these grains has its very own special shape depending on what plant it comes from."

D   "People with allergies know what to expect when the flowers are blooming and the bees are buzzing."

Guided Practice

Read the passage and answer the questions that follow.

Sea Surface Temperature

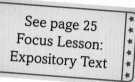

See page 25
Focus Lesson:
Expository Text

1   Less than a century ago, scientists and sailors used buckets to measure sea surface temperatures. Sea surface temperature readings are taken at the top layer of the ocean. Scientists use these temperatures for everything from keeping an eye on ecosystems to predicting El Nino (abnormally warm ocean surface temperatures in the Pacific Ocean) and La Nina (abnormally cold ocean surface temperatures in the Pacific Ocean) events.

2   So, how were buckets used to measure sea surface temperatures? Sailors would lower wooden buckets over the sides of their ships. They dragged them through the water until the buckets were full. Next, the sailors would pull the buckets back up to the ship deck. They put a thermometer into the water and waited for about three minutes. Then they recorded these temperatures in the ship's logbook.

3   As you can probably imagine, these measurements weren't always the most correct. The bucket way of measuring sea surface temperatures often caused sailors to write down lower temperatures. One reason for these incorrect readings was that evaporation happened as the bucket was pulled back onto the ship and while the thermometer was in the water. Evaporation is a cooling process. This means that as water goes from liquid to vapor, it cools the nearby environment.

4   Luckily, as time passed scientists developed better methods for measuring sea surface temperatures. Today, buoys across the oceans regularly report measurements from special machines. This information is beamed to satellites that quickly send the information to scientists. The National Data Buoy Center cares for many coastal buoys in US waters. These buoys range in size from around 5 feet to nearly 40 feet across—nearly seven times the height of the average American male! However, buoys aren't just found in US coastal waters. The National Data Buoy Center also works with several international agencies to measure and watch sea surface temperatures around the globe.

5 Sea surface temperatures affect the behavior of Earth's atmosphere. Studying the temperatures is very important in predicting storms and other weather. Working with scientists around the world, the National Climatic Data Center continues to help measure sea surface temperatures from around the world. This way, scientists and the public have the best available information to predict how the sea surface temperature will affect the environment and the climate.

1 **Part A**

What is the main idea of this article?

_____

_____

_____

> Review the first four paragraphs. How was sea surface temperature measured in the past, and how it is measured today?

Part B

Which sentence supports the main idea you stated in Part A?

_____

_____

_____

> Read paragraphs 1 through 4. Which sentence relates to how sea surface temperature was measured in the past and how it is measured today?

2   Part A

What was the main problem with using buckets to measure sea surface temperature?

_____

_____

> Reread paragraph 3. What happened when sailors used this method to measure temperatures?

Part B

What was the reason for the problem you stated in Part A?

_____

_____

_____

_____

> When measuring temperature with buckets, sailors often wrote down lower temperatures. Why was this?

3   Part A

Why is it important to know the surface temperature of the sea?

_____

_____

_____

> Reread the end of the article. Find out what is influenced by the surface temperature of the sea.

Part B

What might happen if scientists did not know the surface temperature of the sea?

_____

_____

_____

> You have to make an inference here. Use your answer to Part A to help you.

Read the passage and answer the questions that follow.

Miss Mitchell's Comet

by Catherine Mahoney

1   Maria Mitchell was the first American woman to earn a living as an astronomer, a scientist who studies space. Maria was born in 1818, and grew up on the island of Nantucket with her father William, her mother Lydia, and her nine sisters and brothers. William was a teacher, and Lydia was a librarian with a passion for reading—she worked in two circulating libraries, and she had read every book on the shelves of both. Maria, like her mother, spent her time reading. Maria's teacher—who was also her father—quickly concluded that this shy little girl had a brilliant mind.

2   When he wasn't teaching, William studied the heavens above. He even built a small observatory on his own land, so he could better see and learn about the stars. The US Coast Survey paid him one hundred dollars a year for his observations.

3   William believed that his daughters should be as well educated as his sons. He taught Maria the same lessons as his sons and gave her extra instruction in astronomy, which she loved. Unlike other girls of her time, Maria refused to spend time knitting and making lace. She often remarked, "A woman might be learning seven languages while she is learning fancy work."

4   Maria left public school at 16 and attended private school for another year. After this, she assisted her father in his work with the Coast Survey. Because of this work, famous professors often visited the Mitchell home. Maria enjoyed talking to and learning from them.

5   Maria wanted to spend her time studying, but her family needed her to help support them. Maria's older sister earned a good living as a teacher, but Maria chose to work as a librarian at the Nantucket library. While she earned little, the job allowed her to spend her days reading and learning all she could about astronomy. She worked at the library for 20 years.

6   One night in October of 1847, Maria made an important discovery. While gazing through her telescope, she was startled to see an unknown comet. She quickly told her father, who wrote to Professor William C. Bond, director of the Observatory at Cambridge, to ask if anyone had seen this comet before. No one had.

7   Maria was awarded a medal for this discovery and the comet was named "Miss Mitchell's Comet" in her honor. This was not her only accomplishment, however. Aside from being the first American woman to work as an astronomer, Maria was a professor and published several books and many articles.

The Comet ISON

1   People everywhere are talking about ISON. Who—or what—is ISON you ask? It is a comet that is close to the planet Jupiter. Astronomers, scientists who study space, believe that ISON is going to travel very close to the sun. Comets travel in a large circle called an orbit. When a comet gets close to the sun, it becomes bright enough for people to see it without a telescope. ISON's orbit, however, should take it very close to the sun. This will make it extremely hot and bright. People may be able to see ISON in the sky for months.

2   There's another possibility, however. ISON is very far away—470 million miles away. Anything could happen to it on its journey toward the sun. "Comets can and often do fizzle out!" notes Karl Battams of the Sungrazer Comet Project.

3   Two men in Russia who study astronomy as a hobby discovered ISON. They saw the comet using a telescope called the International Scientific Optical Network (ISON), which is how the comet got its name.

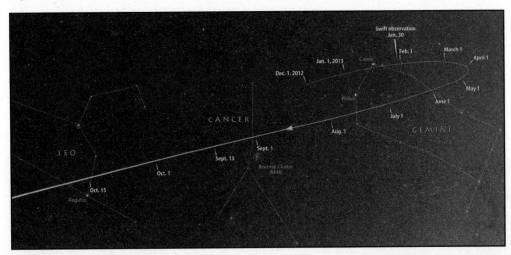

1   Part A

Using information from both articles, what can you conclude about the comet Maria Mitchell saw?

A   It was near Jupiter.

B   It was near the sun.

C   It quickly fizzled out.

D   It could be seen for months.

Part B

Which sentence best supports your answer to Part A?

A   "It is a comet that is close to the planet Jupiter."

B   "Anything could happen to it on its journey toward the sun."

C   "'Comets can and often do fizzle out!' notes Karl Battams of the Sungrazer Comet Project."

D   "When a comet gets close to the sun, it becomes bright enough for people to see it without a telescope."

2   Part A

How did the comet ISON get its name?

A   The comet was named after a telescope.

B   The comet was named after Karl Battams.

C   The comet was named after a place in Russia.

D   The comet was named after two men from Russia.

Part B

Suppose the comet Maria discovered got its name the way ISON did. What would Maria's comet have been named after?

A   the person she admired the most

B   the place she was at when she saw it

C   the person who taught her about comets

D   the telescope she was using when she saw it

3 Part A

Which words best describe Maria Mitchell?

A   curious and faithful

B   brave and interested

C   serious and thoughtful

D   eager and determined

Part B

Which sentence from the passage "Miss Mitchell's Comet" best supports your answer to Part A?

A   "Maria wanted to spend her time studying but her family needed her to help support them."

B   "She often remarked, 'A woman might be learning seven languages while she is learning fancy work.'"

C   "While she earned little, the job allowed her to spend her days reading and learning all she could about astronomy."

D   "He taught Maria the same lessons as his sons and gave her extra instruction in astronomy, which she loved."

Lesson 1

Literary Text focuses on the wonders of the sea and of make-believe through a poem and a play.

 ## Lesson 2

Literary Text focuses on an island in the sea and another in the sky.

 ## Lesson 3

Informational Text focuses on using waste to create a rich soil and on using balloons to learn more about your climate.

 ## Lesson 4

Informational Text shows how astronauts learn to move in space and why and how you need to move your body everyday.

Guided Practice

Read the passage and answer the questions that follow.

Song of the Sea

by Barry Cornwall

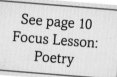
See page 10
Focus Lesson:
Poetry

1   The sea! the sea! the open sea!
    The blue, the fresh, the ever free!
    Without a mark, without a bound,
    It runneth the earth's wide regions round;
    It plays with the clouds; it mocks the skies,
    Or like a cradled creature lies.

2   I'm on the sea! I'm on the sea!
    I am where I would ever be;
    With the blue above and the blue below,
    And silence wheresoe'er I go.
    If a storm should come and awake the deep
    What matter? *I* shall ride and sleep.

3   I love, oh, how I love to ride
    On the fierce, foaming, bursting tide,
    When every mad wave drowns the moon,
    Or whistles aloud his tempest tune,
    And tells how goeth the world below,
    And why the southwest blasts do blow.

4   I never was on the dull, tame shore,
    But I loved the great sea more and more,
    And back I flew to her billowy breast,
    Like a bird that seeketh its mother's nest;
    And a mother she *was*, and *is*, to me,
    For I was born on the open sea!

5   I've lived, since then, in calm and strife,
    Full fifty summers a sailor's life,
    With wealth to spend and a power to range,
    But never have sought nor sighed for change;
    And I know whatever happens to me,
    Shall come on the wild, unbounded sea.

1   Part A

Who is the speaker of this poem?

_____

_____

_____

> Reread stanzas 4 and 5. The speaker reveals his identity near the end of the poem.

Part B

Which line or lines support your answer to Part A?

_____

_____

_____

_____

> Look for the lines in the poem where the speaker says how he has lived since he was born on the sea.

2 Part A

How does the speaker of the poem feel about living on land?

_____

_____

> Read stanza 4 again. What does the speaker say about the shore?

Part B

How does he feel about living on the sea?

_____

_____

> Read stanza 2 again. This is the opposite of how he feels about living on shore.

3   Part A

Suppose this poem were rewritten as a short story. How would it be different?

_____

_____

_____

_____

> Think about how a story is different from a poem. What does a short story have that a poem does not?

Part B

If this poem were rewritten as a short story, who do you think would be the main character and why?

_____

_____

_____

> Who and what is this poem mostly about? The story would be about this person and subject as well.

Warm Winter Surprises

Adapted from *Little Women*
by *Louisa May Alcott*

Cast of Characters

Meg, *age 16, pretty and well-mannered, she has soft brown hair. Like her sisters, she is simply dressed.*

Jo, *age 15, tall, thin, and awkward, she is very active*

Beth, *calm and quiet, age 13, Elizabeth is rosy and tidy and the peacekeeper of the family*

Amy, *the youngest sister, a beauty with blue eyes and curly blonde hair, she is dainty and artistic*

Marmee, *the girls' mother is tall and gentle. She wears a gray cloak, plain bonnet, and practical shoes.*

ACT ONE, Scene 1

The setting is a small New England town during the Civil War. The March sisters gather in a neat but shabby sitting room with a hearth. The room is furnished with an armchair and table and a fire is burning in the fireplace.

The clock strikes six. Amy is sitting in an armchair. Beth sweeps the hearth and puts a pair of old slippers near the fire to warm. Jo and Meg enter the room.

Jo: *(holding the slippers closer to the fire)* These are quite worn out. Marmee must have a new pair.

Beth: I thought I'd get her some with my dollar.

Amy: *(rising from the armchair)* No, I shall!

Meg: I'm the oldest…!

Jo: *(interrupting)* I'm the man of the family now that Papa is away, and I shall provide the slippers, for he told me to take special care of Mother while he was gone.

Beth: I'll tell you what we'll do. Let's each get her something for the holiday instead of buying presents for each other. She'll get more presents this way.

Jo: That's like you, dear! What will we get?

The girls look around, thinking.

Meg: *(looking at her own pretty hands)* I shall give her a nice pair of gloves.

Jo: Army shoes, best to be had!

Beth: Some handkerchiefs, all hemmed. *(She begins toasting bread on a long fork.)*

Amy: I'll get a little bottle of perfume. She likes it, and it won't cost much, so I'll have some left to buy my colored pencils.

Meg: How will we give the things?

Jo: We'll put them on the table, and bring her in and see her open the bundles. We'll let Marmee think we are getting things for ourselves, and then surprise her. We must go shopping tomorrow afternoon, Meg. And there is so much to do about the holiday play. *(She marches about the room, her hands behind her back and her nose in the air.)*

Meg: I don't mean to act any more after this time. I'm getting too old for such things.

Jo: You won't stop, I know, as long as you can trail round in a white gown with your hair down, and wear gold-paper jewelry. You are the best actress we've got, and there'll be an end of everything if you quit. We ought to rehearse tonight. *(turning to Amy)* Come here, Amy, and do the fainting scene, for you are as stiff as a poker in that.

Amy: I can't help it. I never saw anyone faint, and I don't choose to make myself all black and blue, tumbling flat as you do. If I can go down easily, I'll drop. If I can't, I shall fall into a chair and be graceful.

Jo: Do it this way. Clasp your hands, and stagger across the room, crying frantically, 'Roderigo! Save me! Save me!' *(Jo staggers and delivers the lines, screaming.)*

Amy tries to follow her example, but she is stiff and jerky in her movements. Jo shakes her head in despair, while Meg laughs. Beth forgets to watch the bread and burns it.

Jo: It's no use! Do the best you can when the time comes, and if the audience laughs, don't blame me.

The girls continue to laugh as Amy practices her faint.

Marmee: *(entering the room)* Glad to find you so merry, my girls! *(The girls rush to hug her as she removes her wet cloak and shoes.)* Well, dearies, how have you got on today? There was so much to do, getting the boxes ready to go tomorrow, that I didn't come home to dinner. Has anyone called, Beth? How is your cold, Meg? Jo, you look tired to death. Come and kiss me, baby.

Marmee sits in the armchair. The girls bring her warmed slippers, which she slides on. Amy climbs into her lap.

Marmee: *(smiling)* I've got a treat for you. *(She pulls a letter from her pocket.)*

Beth claps her hands, then sits on a chair in the corner.

Jo: A letter! A letter! Three cheers for Father!

Marmee: Yes, a nice long letter, with a message for you girls. *(She reads):* Give them all of my dear love and a kiss. Tell them I think of them by day, pray for them by night, and take comfort in their love for me. A year seems very long to wait before I see them. Remind them that while we wait, we may all work, so that these hard days need not be wasted. I know they will remember all I said to them, that they will be loving children to you, will do their duty faithfully, and behave so beautifully that when I come back to them I may be fonder and prouder than ever of my little women. *(The girls cry, and Amy hides her face on her mother's shoulder.)*

Amy: I am a selfish girl! But I'll truly try to be better.

Meg: We all will!

Beth picks up a half-finished army sock, wipes her tears, and begins to knit quickly.

Jo: I'll try and be what he loves to call me, "a little woman," and not be rough and wild, but do my duty here instead of wanting to be somewhere else.

Marmee hugs and kisses her girls, wiping away tears. The curtain closes.

End of ACT ONE, Scene 1

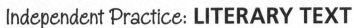

1 Part A

What does Beth suggest that they do for Marmee?

A buy her extra presents

B put her presents on a table

C read her an important letter

D warm her slippers by the fire

Part B

Based on Beth's suggestion, what does Jo want to do?

A buy her gloves

B buy her army shoes

C get a bottle of perfume

D hem some handkerchiefs

2 Part A

Who is going to do the fainting scene in the holiday play?

A Jo

B Meg

C Amy

D Beth

Part B

What is humorous about this?

A She is too old.

B She is too stiff.

C Her gown is too long.

D Her jewelry is made of paper.

3   Part A

How would this drama be different if it were rewritten as a short story?

A   It would have dialogue.

B   It would have a setting.

C   It would have longer stanzas.

D   It would have more description.

Part B

What would be omitted from this drama if it were rewritten as a short story?

A   the plot

B   the setting

C   the stanzas

D   the stage directions

Guided Practice

Read the passage and answer the questions that follow.

The Tempest

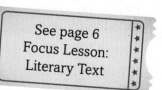

See page 6
Focus Lesson:
Literary Text

1   Prospero, the Duke of Milan, was a scholar who lived among his books. He left the management of his dukedom to his brother Antonio, in whom he had complete trust. But that trust was not well placed, for Antonio wanted to wear the duke's crown himself. To gain the crown, he would have killed his brother—but the people loved Prospero, and Antonio couldn't risk it.

2   However, with the help of Prospero's great enemy, Alonso, King of Naples, he took control of the power and riches of the dukedom. They took Prospero to sea, and when they were far away from land, forced him into a little boat. They put his little daughter, Miranda, not yet 3 years old, into the boat with him, and sailed away, leaving them to their fate.

3   But one man, Gonzalo, was true to his rightful master. To save the duke from his enemies was impossible, but this worthy lord secretly placed fresh water, food, and clothing into the boat. And he put in what Prospero valued most of all, his precious books.

4   The boat landed on an island, and Prospero and his little girl landed safely. Now, this island was enchanted, and for years had lain under the spell of a witch. She had imprisoned all the good spirits she found there in the trunks of trees. When she died, the spirits remained in their prisons.

5   Prospero was a great magician, for he had devoted himself to the study of magic. By magic he set the imprisoned spirits free. But he made them obey him and serve him. He treated them kindly, as long as they did his bidding.

6   Years later, when Miranda had grown into a beautiful maiden, it chanced that Antonio and some other men were at sea together when their ship came near Prospero's island. Prospero, knowing they were there, raised by magic a great storm, so that even the sailors on board gave up hope. One, Prince Ferdinand, leaped into the sea. But the spirit Ariel brought him safely ashore, as well as all the rest of the crew. The good ship herself, which the crew thought had been wrecked, lay at anchor in the harbor, where Ariel had brought her.

7   While the tempest was raging, Prospero showed his daughter the brave ship laboring in the sea, and told her that it was filled with living human beings like themselves. Then, for the first time, he told her the story of his life and hers, and that he had caused this storm so that his enemies, Antonio and Alonso, who were on board, might be delivered into his hands.

8   Prospero sent Ariel in search of the young prince. And Ariel, invisible to Ferdinand, hovered near him, singing a magic song. Ferdinand followed the magic singing and Ariel led the spellbound prince to Prospero and Miranda. Then, all happened as Prospero desired. For Miranda, who had never seen any human being except her father, looked on the youthful prince with reverence in her eyes and love in her secret heart.

9   And Ferdinand, beholding her beauty with wonder and delight, thought she must be a goddess. Scarcely had they exchanged half a dozen sentences, but Ferdinand vowed to make Miranda his queen if she were willing. But Prospero, though secretly delighted, pretended to be angry.

10   "You come here as a spy," he said to Ferdinand. "I will chain your feet together. You shall feed on fresh water mussels, withered roots and husk, and have sea-water to drink. Follow me!"

11   "No," said Ferdinand, and drew his sword. But Prospero put a spell on him, so that he stood there like a statue, still as stone. And Miranda in terror begged her father to have mercy on her prince.

12   But he harshly refused, and made Ferdinand follow him to his house. There he set the prince to work. He made him remove hundreds of heavy logs and pile them up. Ferdinand patiently obeyed, and thought his toil all too well repaid by the sympathy of the sweet Miranda.

13   In pity, she would have helped him in his hard work, but he would not let her. But he could not keep from her the secret of his love, and she, hearing it, was delighted and promised to be his wife.

14   Then Prospero released him from his servitude, and glad at heart, he gave his consent to their marriage.

15   So all ended happily. The ship was safe in the harbor, and next day they all set sail for Naples, where Ferdinand and Miranda would be married. Prospero went back to his dukedom, where he was welcomed with great joy.

16   As for Ariel, Prospero made him free as air, so that he could wander where he would and sing with a light heart.

1 **Part A**

Read this sentence from the passage.

> "Ferdinand patiently obeyed, and thought his toil all too well repaid by the sympathy of the sweet Miranda."

What does the word *toil* mean?

_____

_____

> Read the sentences in paragraph 12 that come before this sentence. How do these sentences help you know the meaning of *toil*?

Part B

Which sentence or sentences helped you to answer the question in Part A?

_____

_____

_____

_____

> Look for a sentence in paragraph 12 that explains what the prince was doing.

2 **Part A**

What does Gonzalo do to help Prospero and Miranda?

_____

_____

_____

> Prospero and Miranda are able to survive in the little boat. Why?

Part B

Why does Gonzalo have to do this in secret?

_____

_____

_____

_____

> Reread paragraph 3. Use the information in this paragraph and your own ideas to answer the question.

Picnic on Sky Island

Adapted from *Sky Island*
by *L. Frank Baum*

1   Mrs. Griffith knew nothing of the flight of the Magic Umbrella. But she never objected when Trot wanted to go with Cap'n Bill for a day's picnicking, for the old sailor cared for Trot better than she did herself. So Trot, remembering that Button-Bright would be with them, loaded the basket with all the good things she could find.

2   By the time she came out, Cap'n Bill and Button-Bright had appeared. "Now then, where'll we go?" asked Trot.

3   "Anywhere suits me," replied Cap'n Bill.

4   Looking far out over the Pacific, the girl's eyes fell upon a dim island lying on the horizon line just where the sky and water seemed to meet.

5   "Oh, Cap'n Bill!" she exclaimed, pointing. "Let's go to Sky Island for our picnic. We've never been there!" After some discussion, the decision was made.

6   "Very well," said Button-Bright. "I want to go to Sky Island!" he said to the umbrella. The umbrella started promptly and rose higher than ever, carrying the three voyagers with it, and then started straight away over the ocean. But it sailed way past the island Trot had asked for. The umbrella made a path through black clouds and into misty, billowy white ones, where they caught sight of a majestic rainbow before diving into another bank of clouds.

7   "Seems to me we're goin' down," called Trot.

8   "Look!" called Cap'n Bill. "There's an island below us. The blue is around one side of it an' pink sunshine around the other side. An' bein' as it's in the sky, it's likely to be Sky Island."

9　"Then we shall land there," said Button-Bright confidently. "I knew the umbrella wouldn't make a mistake."

10　Suddenly, the picnic basket that was dangling below Cap'n Bill struck something with a loud thud, which was followed by a yell of anger.

11　"Get off me! Get off, I say!" cried an excited voice. "What in the Sky do you mean by sitting on my feet? Get off at once!"

12　Button-Bright and Trot were staring at the strangest being they had ever seen. He had two long legs, a body as round as a ball, a neck like an ostrich, and a comical little head set on the top of it. But his skin was sky-blue, his eyes were sky-blue, his hair and his clothes were sky-blue; and on his chest glittered a star-shaped jewel set with splendid blue stones. In fact, everything on the island was the same color blue—the trees, the grass, the flowers, and even the pebbles.

13　But the blue creature would not permit them to look around. As soon as Cap'n Bill stood, the blue man cried, "How dare you come into my garden and fall on my toes? I am the Royal Boolooroo of Sky Island!"

14　"Oh, is this Sky Island, then?" asked Trot.

15　"Of course it's Sky Island. What else could it be? And I'm its Ruler, its King, its sole Royal Potentate and Dictator. You have injured the Mighty Quitey Righty Boolooroo of the Blues!"

16　"Glad to meet you, sir," said Cap'n Bill. "Please 'scuse me for sittin' on your royal toes. I didn't know as your toes were there."

17　"I won't excuse you!" roared the Boolooroo. "I'll punish you!"

18　"You're actin' rather impolite," said Trot. "If anyone comes to our country, we always treat 'em nice."

19　"YOUR country!" exclaimed the Boolooroo. "Where in the Sky did you come from, then, and where is your country?"

20　"We live on the Earth," replied Trot.

21　"The Earth? Nonsense! Earth isn't inhabited—no one can live there. It's just a round, cold ball of mud and water," declared the Blueskin.

22　"I feel sorry for you," replied Trot, "'cause you don't know how to treat visitors. But we'll go home pretty soon."

23　"Not until you have been punished!" exclaimed the Boolooroo sternly. "You are my prisoners."

24 As a matter o' fact, Your Majesty," said Cap'n Bill, "we've captured your whole bloomin' blue island, but we don't like the place very much, so as soon as we eat a bite of lunch, we'll sail away."

25 "Sail away? How?" asked the Boolooroo.

26 "With the Magic Umbrella," said Cap'n Bill, pointing to the umbrella that Button-Bright was holding.

27 "Oh, ho! I see, I see," said the Boolooroo, nodding his funny head. "Go ahead, then, and eat your lunch."

28 But he watched the strangers carefully. Cap'n Bill whispered that they must eat and get away quickly. Trot longed to see more of the strange blue island, but she felt that her old friend was wise in advising them to leave. So she opened the basket, and they all sat in a row on a blue stone bench and began to eat all the good things that were packed in the lunch basket.

1 Part A

What is the theme of this story?

A It is better to be safe than sorry.

B It is better to be polite than rude.

C A magic umbrella is a good way to travel.

D You should stand up for what you think is right.

Part B

Which sentence from the story best supports your answer to Part A?

A "Cap'n Bill whispered that they must eat and get away quickly."

B "'I feel sorry for you,' replied Trot, ' 'cause you don't know how to treat visitors.'"

C "'With the Magic Umbrella,' said Cap'n Bill, pointing to the umbrella that Button-Bright was holding."

D "'You're actin' rather impolite,' said Trot. 'If anyone comes to our country, we always treat 'em nice.'"

2 Part A

Which word from the story best describes Boolooroo, the blue creature on Sky Island?

A ugly

B mean

C curious

D surprised

Part B

Which sentence from the story best supports your answer to Part A?

A "'What in the Sky do you mean by sitting on my feet?'"

B "'I won't excuse you!' roared the Boolooroo. 'I'll punish you!'"

C "'Where in the Sky did you come from, then, and where is your country?'"

D "Button-Bright and Trot were staring at the strangest being they had ever seen."

3   Part A

Read this sentence from the story.

"But the blue creature would not permit them to look around."

What does the word *permit* mean?

A   help

B   allow

C   accept

D   support

Part B

Which sentence from the story helped you determine the answer to Part A?

A   "'I am the Royal Boolooroo of Sky Island!'"

B   "'Get off me! Get off, I say!' cried an excited voice."

C   "As soon as Cap'n Bill stood, the blue man cried, 'How dare you come into my garden and fall on my toes?'"

D   "In fact, everything on the island was the same color blue—the trees, the grass, the flowers, and even the pebbles."

Guided Practice

Read the passage and answer the questions that follow.

Build Your Own Compost Pile

See page 22
Focus Lesson:
Instructional Text

1 Have you ever wondered how you can change garbage into treasure? If you said "Composting," you would be correct!

2 Because landfills are filling up so quickly, it is up to us to find new ways to get rid of our garbage. About 30 percent of all the garbage in the United States is made up of waste from food and backyards. Composting is a great way to recycle household and lawn waste. This waste includes grass clippings, eggshells, and orange peels. Composting is a biological process that occurs when tiny organisms break down old plant and animal tissues and recycle them to make new, healthy soil. These old plant and animal tissues are often called organic wastes.

Before You Begin

3 To create a compost pile, you will need to gather some tools, as well as educate yourself about composting.

4 Composting is not a difficult process. You don't even need many tools. However, you should gather the following before you get started:

- Shovel
- Composting pail
- Gardening gloves
- Watering hose

5 In addition to these items, you may want to consider other composting materials such as organic fertilizer, specialty worms, or dried hay. To find composting supplies, please visit your local garden products dealer or home and garden store.

Location

6 Setting up a compost pile can be very easy if you are ready to do a little work! The first step is to select a location for your compost pile. You can put it anywhere in your backyard except near the house or a fence. If your

pile is too close to your house, the worms and organisms that will live in the pile may get into your house! Yuck! So make sure you have plenty of room to work around. You may also want to be sure that your garden hose reaches the spot where you are working since you will need to water it occasionally. The pile should be at least 3 feet wide by 3 feet deep by 3 feet tall. If it is much smaller or larger, it won't compost correctly!

Compost Pile or Bin?

7   You can either build your pile on the ground or buy a special bin to contain the pile. Check with your parents to decide which option is best for you.

8   Using a bin can help your pile to look neater and will work faster. You can also buy special bins so that you can compost inside your house! There are many different kinds of bins that you can buy or even make yourself!

Compost Recipe

9   Now that you have a location and perhaps a container in which to store your pile, what should you put in it? Your "recipe" for great compost is made up of two basic things: green stuff and brown stuff. Green stuff is materials like grass clippings, lettuce scraps, weeds, and other plant wastes. These green materials have high amounts of the element nitrogen. The compost pile needs nitrogen to help the microorganisms work properly. In addition to nitrogen, you also need plenty of the element carbon in your compost pile. Carbon gives the microorganisms energy to do their jobs. Carbon is found in brown stuff such as leaves and pine needles.

10   There are a few no-no's in composting. You should not put the following materials in your compost pile:

- Meat scraps

- Bones

- Dairy products such as milk, cheese, or ice cream

- Oily foods

11   These products attract rodents and may cause the compost pile to stink! Yuck! You can put small scraps of newspaper in your pile because it is biodegradable. You can also throw in droppings from small animals such as hamsters and gerbils.

Building the Compost Pile

12 To build the best possible compost pile, follow these steps:

- First, use the garden hose to wet the ground under the pile

- Place some small twigs or leaves at the bottom (brown stuff). This will help the pile get oxygen later.

- Add your organic wastes now (green stuff)! Be sure to keep the pile somewhat damp as you are adding materials.

- Add some soil to the pile. This layer contains the microorganisms and worms that will help make the compost.

- Put more leaves, hay, or very small twigs (brown stuff) on the top of the pile.

Taking Care of your Pile

13 In a few days, your pile should become very warm inside. It can reach temperatures of between 90 to 140 degrees within 4 to 5 days. You may even see steam rising from it! You should use your shovel or pitchfork to mix up and turn the pile every few days. This will help the tiny organisms and worms work on the entire pile. Also, make sure that the pile has plenty of moisture without getting too wet. If you pick up a pile of the dirt and squeeze it, a few drops of water should come out.

1 Part A

What two types of waste are recycled during composting?

_____

_____

_____

_____

> Look at the section under the heading "Compost Recipe." What waste does the author call "green stuff"? What is "brown stuff"?

Part B

What materials should not be put in a compost pile?

_____

_____

_____

_____

> The author says that some materials smell and attract rodents. These materials should not be put in a compost pile. What products are these?

2   Part A

What elements should you have in your compost pile?

_____

_____

_____

> Reread the section "Compost Recipe." What gases should you have in your compost pile?

Part B

Why do you need these elements in your compost pile?

_____

_____

_____

> In the "Compost Recipe" section, the author explains why these elements are important. There is something in the compost pile that needs these elements to survive. What depends on these elements to do their work?

3 Part A

What is a good location for a compost pile?

_____

_____

_____

> Reread the information under the subheading "Location." What does it say about picking a place to put your compost pile?

Part B

Why does the author tell you to build a compost pile away from a house or fence?

_____

_____

_____

_____

> Use the information in the passage and your own ideas to answer this question.

Read the passage and answer the questions that follow.

Balloons Aren't Just for Birthdays

1   What's that in the sky? Is it a bird? Is it a plane? No, it's a National Oceanic and Atmospheric Administration (NOAA) weather balloon! Balloons aren't just for birthday parties. They also help scientists learn about weather and climate all over the world.

2   Every day, NOAA's National Weather Service launches large hydrogen- or helium-filled balloons from more than 100 sites throughout the United States, the Caribbean, and the Pacific. As these balloons rise through the atmosphere, equipment on a small machine measures air pressure, temperature, water vapor, and winds from Earth's surface up to about 20 miles high in the sky. The equipment is linked to a battery-powered radio transmitter, which sends the measurements to a ground-tracking receiver.

3   When the balloons are first released, they are about 5 feet wide. They gradually expand as they rise because the air pressure decreases. When the balloon is high enough and the pressure is low enough, it swells until it bursts. A small, orange parachute then slows the descent of the instrument. This makes it less likely that the balloon will hurt anyone or damage property on the ground. An average weather balloon will stay afloat for more than two hours. It may drift about 180 miles from where it was first released. If the weather balloon enters a strong wind current, it can travel at speeds greater than 250 mph.

4   The National Weather Service uses the data collected by weather balloons to study and predict changes in the atmosphere. The data help forecasters identify and warn the public and pilots of severe weather. It also helps check satellite data and information for weather forecasting models. NCDC keeps these data in the center's weather balloon data archive. The data provides valuable information for weather and climate change research. This information keeps people safe from powerful storms.

5   Measurement machines and their attached flight equipment are safe to touch, even though they sometimes make strange noises or smell funny. Each weather balloon machine has its own addressed, postage-paid return mailbag. So, if you find a weather balloon or its equipment, please return it to the sender. Returning the machines helps the environment and saves money by recycling the units.

1   Part A

How wide are the balloons when they are first released into the air?

A   5 feet

B   10 feet

C   50 feet

D   100 feet

Part B

What makes the balloons expand?

A   an increase in air pressure

B   a decrease in air pressure

C   an increase in temperature

D   a decrease in temperature

2   Part A

What is released from a weather balloon after it bursts?

A   a small satellite

B   a small parachute

C   a ground receiver

D   a radio transmitter

Part B

Based on your answer to Part A, why is this released?

A   to warn the public

B   to measure the wind

C   to slow down the balloon

D   to keep the balloon afloat

3 **Part A**

Read this sentence from paragraph 4.

"The data provides valuable information for weather and climate research."

What does the word *valuable* mean as it is used here?

A new

B basic

C important

D expensive

Part B

Which sentence from the article best supports your answer to Part A?

A "This information keeps people safe from powerful storms."

B "NCDC keeps these data in the center's weather balloon data archive."

C "It also helps check satellite data and information for weather forecasting models."

D "The data help forecasters identify and warn the public and pilots of severe weather."

Guided Practice

Read the passage and answer the questions that follow.

Spacewalk Training

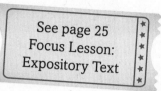

See page 25
Focus Lesson:
Expository Text

1   As much fun as it is just to go to space, being able to go outside your spacecraft is even more exciting. However, before you can float out the door into space, you must spend many hours learning how to do a spacewalk, or extravehicular activity (EVA).

2   The 280-pound spacesuit is the first obstacle you must conquer. For starters, you must learn how to put it on. The spacesuit provides you with the air you need to breathe while you're outside your spacecraft. It also keeps your body at a comfortable temperature, even though it may be anywhere from 200 degrees below zero to 200 degrees above zero outside. Because the suit is so large, you must practice moving around while wearing it, and learn how to use tools with bulky gloves on your hands. Astronauts practice spacewalking in large pools. They usually spend seven hours training underwater for every hour they will spend spacewalking during a mission.

3   Astronauts train to use US spacesuits in the Neutral Buoyancy Laboratory (NBL) at the Johnson Space Center in Houston, Texas. The NBL is a huge pool filled with 6.2 million gallons of water. In fact, it's the world's largest indoor pool—202 feet long, 102 feet wide, and 40 feet deep. At the bottom of the NBL sits a model of the International Space Station, which is the same size as the one orbiting Earth—that's why the NBL needs to be so big. A model of the space shuttle's bay is also located here.

4   Being underwater in a pool is a lot like being in space, but not exactly the same. You're not truly weightless in a pool as you are in space. In the NBL, weights or floats are attached to your spacesuit. This makes you feel much like you will in space, when you're floating free without gravity.

5   You will begin your training by going through your planned spacewalks while wearing regular scuba gear. Once you've gotten comfortable with all the tasks you will perform, you will start practicing them while wearing your spacesuit. In the pool, scuba divers will help you move around until you get used to moving in your spacesuit. They're also there to protect you in case you have a problem with your suit. You'll also learn how to stay in one

place—don't push too hard in space or you'll float away! Next, you'll learn how to use all the tools you'll need during your spacewalk. If you're going to help build the International Space Station, for example, you will practice only the tasks you will do in space. You will practice every task dozens of times before you ever leave Earth. You will practice until you can do it correctly every time. If you're going to be part of a space station *Expedition* crew, you will learn how to do many tasks outside the space station, so you'll be ready to fix anything that might break.

6   By the time you're ready to fly into space, you will have spent more than 100 hours underwater practicing for your spacewalks. When the time comes to put on your suit and float out the door into the vacuum of space for the very first time, you'll know you're ready. And while you're outside, don't forget to take some time to enjoy the view. You will remember that first sight of Earth through your helmet faceplate for the rest of your life.

1   Part A

Why do astronauts learn to spacewalk underwater in a pool?

_____

_____

_____

> Read paragraphs 3 and 4 again. What happens when you are in water?

Part B

How is being in a pool different from being in space?

_____

_____

> The author says being underwater in a pool is a lot like being in space, but not exactly the same. Find the reason why.

2   Part A

What organizational structure does the author use in paragraph 5?

_____

_____

_____

> Read paragraph 5 again. Some common organizational structures used in nonfiction include problem/solution, cause/effect, chronological (also called sequential), and comparison. Is one of these used in the paragraph?

Part B

How do you know your answer to Part A is correct?

_____

_____

_____

_____

> Explain why you chose this answer. Are there any signal words that helped you recognize the structure the author used?

3 Part A

What is one way scuba divers help astronauts who are learning to spacewalk in a pool?

_____

_____

_____

> Reread paragraph 5. Choose one way that scuba divers help astronauts when they are in the pool.

Part B

What is another way that scuba divers help astronauts?

_____

_____

_____

> Go back to paragraph 5 and find the second task they perform to help astronauts.

Let's Move!

Move Every Day!

1   Kids need 60 minutes of moderate to vigorous active play every day. It may sound like a lot, but it doesn't need to happen at one time. Physical activity throughout the day adds up. When you get moving, you're more likely to:

- Feel less stressed.
- Feel better about yourself.
- Feel more ready to learn in school.
- Keep a healthy weight.
- Build and keep healthy bones, muscles and joints.
- Sleep better at night.
- Plan fun activities

2   Use a calendar to set healthy goals every day of the week. Plan activities with your family like swimming, tennis, basketball, Frisbee, or come up with your own ideas to get moving.

Fun Ways to Break up TV Time

3   The average child spends more time watching television, and less time running and playing than in the past. It's important to find creative ways to exercise and play every day, which can be both fun and beneficial to your health. Quiet time for reading and homework is fine, but you should limit time spent watching TV, playing video games, or surfing the web so you have more time to play! If you're going to watch television or play computer games, break it up! Pause the game. Make commercial breaks *Let's Move!* breaks. Here are some active and fun ideas:

- Jumping jacks
- Dancing
- Racing up and down the stairs
- Sit-ups
- Stretching
- Jogging in place
- Push-ups
- Active house chores

Try a New Fruit or Veggie

4   People often don't eat healthy food. Bodies need nutrients—like vitamins, minerals, proteins and carbohydrates—to grow up healthy. You can help your body grow and stay healthy by eating lots of fruits and vegetables. And have fun with this! You can prepare fruits and vegetables in many, delicious ways

Have Fun with Fruit

5   Fruits have important nutrients to keep your body healthy. Here are a few ideas of how to enjoy more fruit, more often:

- Grab an apple for a quick snack. Try different types like red delicious, gala, fuji or granny smith—there are over 7,500 varieties of apples worldwide!

- Join your parents on food shopping trips. Ask to try new fruits like peaches, cantaloupe, pears, and kiwi—there are a lot of sweet and delicious fruits that you can have fun tasting.

- Make a fruit salad with a mix of strawberries, oranges, grapes, and pineapple—or whatever else you have in the house.

- Mix it up! Blend frozen fruit, juice, and low-fat or fat-free yogurt to make a healthy shake that tastes great.

- Top cereal, oatmeal, or toast with strawberries, blueberries, or bananas.

- Drink 100% juice without added sugar—try fresh orange or apple juice.

Take The President's Challenge

Sign up for the President's Challenge at www.presidentschallenge.org, and get into the program by jumping rope, playing catch, or racing a friend. Even better, you can win awards from the President for staying active and track your progress along with kids across America. The more you keep at it, the more fun you'll have.

Vary Your Veggies

6   Vegetables have the vitamins, minerals, and fiber your body needs to grow up healthy. Here are some simple ideas to eat more veggies everyday:

- Snack on veggies like baby carrots, cucumber slices, and celery sticks.

- Keep it colorful—make a salad with a variety of veggies, like corn, carrots, and spinach!

- Join your parents on food shopping trips and choose new veggies like sweet potatoes, beets, red pepper, or sugar snap peas—have fun exploring colorful varieties, learning about what's in season and tasting new foods.

- Try mixing vegetables into your favorite foods. For instance, order a veggie pizza with toppings like mushrooms, green peppers, and onions—ask for extra veggies.

1 Part A

According to the passage, how can you give your body more fiber?

A   Eat more fruit.

B   Drink more juice.

C   Eat more vegetables.

D   Eat more carbohydrates.

Part B

Based on your answer to Part A, which of these would most likely contain the most fiber?

A   a salad

B   a potato

C   a slice of bread

D   a sweetened drink

2 Part A

What organizational structure does the author use in paragraph 3?

A   comparison

B   cause/effect

C   chronological

D   problem/solution

Part B

What other paragraph has this organizational structure?

A   paragraph 1

B   paragraph 2

C   paragraph 4

D   paragraph 5

3 Part A

According to the article, what is a main goal of the President's Challenge?

A   to help kids win awards

B   to help kids have more fun

C   to encourage kids to exercise

D   to encourage kids to eat healthier

Part B

Based on your answer to Part A, what is something you might do if you participate in the President's Challenge?

A   Make a new friend.

B   Eat a salad with dinner.

C   Play catch after school.

D   Drink lot of water each day.

UNIT 4 Land, Sea, and Sky   181

Glossary

Act	a division of a play
Alliteration	when the same or a similar beginning consonant sound is repeated in a line
Antonyms	words with opposite meanings
Autobiography	a story of a person's life written by that subject

Biography	a story of a person's life written by someone other than the subject

Cast	a list of characters in a drama or play
Cause	the reason something happens
Characters	the people in a story or play
Compare	how two things are alike
Contrast	how two things are different
Convince	to make someone feel sure

Definitions	words that tell what another word means
Descriptions	words that tell you more about another word
Dialogue	what the characters say in a story or play
Drama	a story written to be performed

Editorial	an article that gives someone's opinion
Effect	the result or thing that happens

Fable	a short story in which animals act like humans
Fact	a statement or information that can be proven
Fairy Tale	a type of traditional story that involves magical creatures interacting with humans in good and bad ways
Fiction	a made-up story
Folktale	a story about ordinary people that teaches a lesson about how people behave

	Free Verse	a poem that does not rhyme or have a rhythm
G	**Genre**	type of literature
I	**Illustrations**	pictures
	Inferences	information figured out with details from the story and what you know
L	**Legend**	a tale from the past about people and events, usually connected to a specific place or time
	Limerick	a humorous rhyming five-line poem
	Lyric Poem	a poem that expresses the poet's feelings
M	**Main Idea**	what the story, article, or paragraph is about
	Metaphor	a type of figurative language that compares two unlike things but does not use the words *like* or *as*
	Myth	a story that explains something about nature or a people's customs or beliefs
N	**Narrative Poem**	a poem that tells a story
	Narrator	the person who tells the story or describes the events to an audience
	Nonfiction	a story that is true
O	**Onomatopoeia**	words that sound like what they are describing
	Opinion	something that someone believes or thinks
P	**Personal Essay**	a piece of writing in which a person describes and reflects upon something important in that person's life
	Personification	giving human characteristics to something that is not human
	Play	a story written to be performed on a stage
	Plot	a series of events that occur in a story
	Poetry	a story full of musical language with rhyming or rhythm
	Point of View	the opinion of who is telling the story

First-person		the main character is telling the story; uses first-person pronouns *I* and *we*
Third-person		narrator is limited to knowledge of the thoughts and feelings of only one of the characters; uses third-person pronouns *he, she,* and *they*
Prediction		what you think the outcome will be
Prefix		part of a word added to beginning of another word that changes the meaning of the word
Props		objects used by characters on stage

Realistic Fiction	a made-up story that could happen in real life
Rhyme	repeated sounds at the ends of words
Rhythm	pattern of stressed and unstressed beats in a line of poetry

Scene	a division of an act of a play
Scenery	the background and props that create the setting of a play
Script	the written version of a play
Setting	the time and place in which a story or play takes place
Sequence	the order in which things happen
Sidebar	short box printed on the side of the text that has additional information
Simile	a type of figurative language that compares two unlike things using the words *as* or *like*
Stage Directions	advice on how actors should move or speak in a play
Stanza	a group of lines within a poem, similar to a chapter within a book; verse
Suffix	part of a word added to the end of another word that changes the meaning of the word
Summary	a short restatement of the ideas in a passage
Synonyms	words that have a similar meaning

Tall Tale	a traditional story that wildly exaggerates the skills or strengths of a hero
Theme	the message or main idea of a story
Tone	the mood or feeling of a story